DAYS OF HEAVEN ON EARTH

A GUIDE TO THE DAYS AHEAD

BY KEVIN L. ZADAI

www.xulonpress.com

Table of Contents

Author's Note and Special Thanks vii

Chapter 1: *The Promise of Heaven on Earth* 9

Chapter 2: *The Personality of Jesus* 25

Chapter 3: *Your Relationship with Him* 37

Chapter 4: *When Heaven Arrives: Holy Spirit, Glory,*
and Angels 55

Chapter 5: *Phase One: Revelation* 68

Chapter 6: *Phase Two: Visitation* 94

Chapter 7: *Phase Three: Habitation* 114

Chapter 8: *Enoch, the Bride, and the Church Age* 133

Conclusion 149

Author's Note and Special Thanks

In addition to sharing my story with everyone through the book, *Heavenly Visitation: A Guide to Participating in the Supernatural*, the Lord commissioned me to produce *Days of Heaven on Earth: A Guide to the Days Ahead*, a detailed study and account in the areas that Jesus reviewed and revealed to me during several visitations. I want to thank everyone who has encouraged me, assisted me, and prayed for me during the writing of this work including my Pastors, Nathanael and Michelle Wolf, and Dr. Jesse and Cathy Duplantis. Special thanks to my wife Kathi, for her love and dedication to the Lord and me. Special thanks as well to all my friends who know how to pray and get Heaven to Earth and also to get those of the Earth to go to Heaven. A special thanks to Heidi Darst for her awesome job with the editing.

Thanks, Dawn Kopp, for defending the well that so many will now drink from. SHAMMAH!

"THE LORD IS PRESENT"

This book is dedicated to the One Who gave it to me, Jesus Christ the Author and Finisher of my faith. May it be returned to the spot on the bookshelf in Heaven from which it came before it was handed to me!

CHAPTER 1

The Promise of
Heaven on Earth

THE TIME IS NOW

Let's look at an interesting passage from Deuteronomy that I feel is a good place to start our discovery of Days of Heaven on Earth:

> Therefore shall ye lay up these my words in your heart and in your soul, and bind them for a sign upon your hand, that they may be as frontlets between your eyes. And ye shall teach them your children, speaking of them when thou sittest in thine house, and when thou walkest by the way, when thou liest down,

and when thou risest up. And thou shalt write them upon the door posts of thine house, and upon thy gates: That your days may be multiplied, and the days of your children, in the land which the LORD sware unto your fathers to give them, as the days of Heaven upon the earth. For if ye shall diligently keep all these commandments which I command you, to do them, to love the LORD your God, to walk in all his ways, and to cleave unto him; Then will the LORD drive out all these nations from before you, and ye shall possess greater nations and mightier than yourselves. Every place where on the soles of your feet shall tread shall be yours: from the wilderness and Lebanon, from the river, the river Euphrates, even unto the uttermost sea shall your coast be. There shall no man be able to stand before you: for the LORD your God shall lay the fear of you and the dread of you upon all the land that ye shall tread upon, as he hath said unto you. Behold, I set before you this day a blessing and a curse; A blessing, if ye obey the commandments of the LORD your God, which I command you this day (Deuteronomy 11:18–27 KJV, emphasis added).

KEEPING THE WORD BEFORE YOU

We need to keep the words God has spoken to us in full view as much as possible. Moses quoted the Lord in the above passage when He said, "And ye shall teach them to your children, speaking of them when thou sittest in thine house, and when thou walkest by the way, when thou liest down, and when thou risest up. And thou shalt write them upon the door posts of thine house, and upon thy gates." That covers almost everything during our day! This passage shows us clearly that God wants us to know and remember the words He has spoken to us.

The Spirit of God takes what God the Father and Jesus have said and supernaturally reveals those words and their meaning's significance to us. This is the Spirit's work. He will also remind us of all that was spoken in the past by God as it now becomes our present remedy in any situation. The Spirit can also reveal the future and make it our present remedy in preparation to disarm our enemy before the situation or attack even develops.

The apostle Paul spoke of renewing our minds as well as guarding our minds in spiritual warfare. The Word of God is

11

quick and powerful; It is able to divide between what is our soul (mind, will, and emotions) and our spirit (the eternal you) that is created in the image of God (see Hebrews 4:12). When you were born again at conversion, your spirit became a new creature (see 2 Corinthians 5:17).

First, let us discuss renewing our minds. Paul teaches this in his letter to the Romans:

> I beseech you therefore, brethren, by the mercies of God, that you present your bodies a living sacrifice, holy, acceptable to God, which is your reasonable service. And do not be conformed to this world, but be transformed by the *renewing of your mind*, that you may prove what is that good and acceptable and perfect will of God (Romans 12:1–2, emphasis added).

I personally do not believe that you can teach too much about mind renewal. The enemy constantly bombards us with an anti-Christ agenda and mindset via the media's world view, potentially forming an "anti-Christ" mindset in its audience. If you do not actively renew your mind by educating yourself in matters of God by the Spirit and the Word of God, you have already fallen victim to this mindset. There is no neutral ground! If you are in "neutral" you are going downstream fast. We must resist the enemy by renewing our minds. Paul gave us special promises if we would renew our mind. He mentions the words "good", "acceptable," and "the perfect will of God." I know that is what you want; that is what I want as well. The Word of God is food for our inner man, but it is also correction and discipline for our minds. Just think of your mind as a computer: whatever information you install, whatever parameters you set, that is what you will retrieve. You do not expect your computer to do something that you have not programed it to do. Our minds can be trained with the proper responses and parameters for life and Godliness.

Remember, we can feed our spirits with the Word of God but we must also discipline and renew our minds by the Word as well.

The apostle Paul tells the Corinthians that spiritual warfare involves pulling down strongholds of the mind:

> For though we walk in the flesh, we do not war according to the flesh. For the weapons of our warfare are not carnal but mighty in God for pulling down strongholds, casting down arguments and every high thing that exalts

itself against the knowledge of God, bringing every thought into captivity to the obedience of Christ, and being ready to punish all disobedience when your obedience is fulfilled (2 Corinthians 10:3–6).

Paul exposes the dark ploy of the enemy against us: deceit. Demons lie and deceive because that is their mode of operation. They are like their father the devil. He is the "father of lies" and has been lying from the beginning:

Why do you not understand My speech? Because you are not able to listen to My word. You are of your father the devil, and the desires of your father you want to do. He was a murderer from the beginning, and does not stand in the truth, because there is no truth in him. When he speaks a lie, he speaks from his own resources, for he is a liar and the father of it. But because I tell the truth, you do not believe Me (John 8:43–45, emphasis added).

Supernaturally, we can pull down demonic strongholds by using spiritual weapons of truth (sword of the Spirit, which is the Word of God) and bring down anything a demon says that exalts itself above the knowledge of God! Our weapons are not carnal. We should use the example of Jesus, Who used the Word of God against the devil in the desert during His temptation. He responded every time with, "It is written" (see Matthew 4:1–11).

> *Jesus is our Victorious Warrior Who went before us to conquer Satan. We must remember to do what He does. He was the Son of God and the Son of man. In temptation He said, "It is written," to the enemy and we should do the same.*

LOVE THE LORD YOUR GOD

How do we love God? Let us explore what the Bible says about it. Sometimes we realize that what we thought was love were just feelings in our soul (mind, will, and emotions) not deep rooted in our heart (spirit). Peter spoke out of his mind and emotions, but could not deliver when hard pressed in difficult situations because his love commitment needed to be deeper in his heart:

> Then Jesus said to them, "All of you will be made to stumble because of Me this night, for

it is written, 'I will strike the Shepherd, And the sheep of the flock will be scattered.'

But after I have been raised, I will go before you to Galilee." Peter answered and said to Him, "Even if all are made to stumble because of You, I will never be made to stumble." Jesus said to him, "Assuredly, I say to you that this night, before the rooster crows, you will deny Me three times." Peter said to Him, "Even if I have to die with You, I will not deny You!" And so said all the disciples (Matthew 26:31–35).

Peter denied Him three times that night, just as Jesus had prophesied. After His resurrection, Jesus questioned Peter about his love for Him:

So when they had eaten breakfast, Jesus said to Simon Peter, "Simon, son of Jonah, do you love Me more than these?" He said to Him, "Yes, Lord; You know that I love You." He said to him, "Feed My lambs." He said to him again a second time, "Simon, son of Jonah, do you love Me?" He said to Him, "Yes, Lord; You know that I love You." He said to him, "Tend My sheep." He said to him the third time, "Simon, son of Jonah, do you love Me?" Peter was grieved because He said to him the third time, "Do you love Me?" And he said to Him, "Lord, You know all things; You know that I love You." Jesus said to him, "Feed My sheep" (John 21:15–17, emphasis added).

I use this passage to gauge the depth of my love, based on my commitment and not on feelings. I realized that love for God is much deeper than I had known. This has to be revealed to you by the Spirit. How many of us would yield to self-preservation instead of our commitment to Him? I have to evaluate my love walk every day.

I met Jesus when I passed to the other side in 1992 during a surgery (see my book *Heavenly Visitation*). His love for me was so evident that day. He spent time explaining to me what He had done for every person ever born. During my time with Him, I learned the price He paid for me to live forever with Him in His Kingdom. He reminisced about the day in which He had thought of me and spoke me into existence. He put me in my mother's womb. Yes! I was just a thought and He breathed me into a womb. He watched my body form in my mother's womb (see Psalms 139:16 NLT)! Then, as He looked at me at the end of my life in that operating room in 1992, He marveled that I turned out just the way He had spoken. I had a revelation of His Love for me. This experience is the foundation for my discussion on our love for God. We cannot truly love God until we first have a revelation of His love for us. He has a purpose for everyone. He created you and He loves you deeply!

I hesitated in writing this very personal account, but was compelled to share my experiences in hopes that it would help someone. I have had some of the most amazing visits with Jesus. What I am about to share with you is sacred. After the 1992 encounter when I died on the operating table, Jesus returned to me at least once every two years to teach me in person. Each time He returned, He showed me another side of Himself that I had not understood fully. He gave Scriptural support to me as well as taught me on everything I saw and heard. It's nice to *hear* someone say they love you, but sometimes we need to *be shown* that love.

I was in my Seattle home with my wife sleeping early one morning. Around 3 a.m., I awoke and looked to my left towards the dresser in the bedroom. I saw a man in a white robe standing there facing toward the west. Physically he stood three to four feet from my bed facing the west wall where my dresser was. Although still very dark, a light glow in the room showed that it was Jesus. He was looking up and I could see His left side by the way He was facing. He had long hair down to the middle of his back and He stood facing the wall, looking up with His hands folded in front, listening to someone who was speaking to Him. All at once, Jesus knew that I was looking at Him. He turned to me and motioned for me to come and stand with Him. I got up out of bed and stood with Him on his left. I knew this was a very solemn and serious moment, so I folded my hands in front of me and looked up as well. The wall and the ceiling disappeared and a huge judge's bench was before me. I could not see the top of it, but I could hear the rumbling of the Judge sitting on his bench. The dialogue was not in English, so I did not understand the language. Everything shook when the Judge spoke. I knew He was the Father God, but I was not allowed to see Him. The syncopation of the sentence structure indicated He was reading a contract with all kinds of terms that had to be agreed upon in order for the contract to be activated. After a while, I felt the need to ask Jesus what was going on because I could not understand the language, nor did I know why it was so solemn and holy. Jesus looked as if He had been crying when I looked toward Him to ask in what we were participating. Before I could speak, Jesus turned to me crying. His eyes were full of passion and love for me. In a broken voice, He was able to tell me in English what was going on. He said, "I just bought you! You are Mine." He said this all to me while weeping. I couldn't look away, even though what poured from Him overwhelmed me, as if

I were merely a teacup into which He poured the contents of His million gallon storage tank.

The words He spoke to me contained millions of gallons of love and passion, and I couldn't look away! I had to drink it.

His love saturated and overflowed me with passion that I had no ability to comprehend or store within me. At this point my spirit burst into the power of the Resurrection and the room brightened. Receiving His love necessitated physical healing—I was thrown back into my body, which lay on the bed three feet away. When I re-entered my body, I immediately sat up. The room was lit brightly, and I could see an angel standing beside my wife on the other side of the bed. What radiated from me was so bright even the angel gasped, waking my wife. She could not see the angel was beside her. The angel acted as though he had not seen my human spirit illuminate so extremely bright ever before. They do not understand salvation as we do. They long to look into these things, but do not understand. I knew instantly that that angel caught a glimpse of what God had done for man through Jesus Christ. My experience compels me to implore each of you to *believe and do all* that the Lord has commanded you. He said that if you love Him, you will obey His commands. The greatest command is to love one another as well as loving the Lord your God with all your heart. Jesus says:

"If you love Me, keep My commandments. And I will pray the Father, and He will give you another Helper, that He may abide with you forever—the Spirit of truth, whom the world cannot receive, because it neither sees Him nor knows Him; but you know Him, for He dwells with you and will be in you. I will not leave you orphans; I will come to you. A little while longer and the world will see Me no more, but you will see Me. Because I live, you will live also. At that day you will know that I am in My Father, and you in Me, and I in you. He who has My commandments and keeps them, it is he who loves Me. And he who loves Me will be loved by My Father, and I will love him and manifest Myself to him." Judas (not Iscariot) said to Him, "Lord, how is it that You will manifest Yourself to us, and not to the world?" Jesus answered and said to him, *"If anyone loves Me, he will keep My word; and My Father will love him, and We will come to him and make Our home with him.* He who does not love Me does not keep My words; and the word which you hear is not Mine but the Fathers who sent Me (John 14:15–24, emphasis added).

Allow the love of the Father and the Son to permeate
you fully as you receive your healing. Revelation from
the Holy Spirit confirms His truth to you in the name
of Jesus! The Father and the Son will come and make
Their home with you. Open your heart's door and
watch Them move in to stay!

WALK IN ALL HIS WAYS

Faith is necessary to believe and trust that God's will and plans for you are the best. Not all of us understand the reality of that truth yet. The Spirit of God wants everyone to know that His ways are *reality*. That is what the word "truth" means. I have learned that He has amazing plans for people. These plans are written down in Heaven and they are classified as truth. Let's look at the next prerequisite for Heaven on Earth-Walking in His Ways. King David comments:

Keep trusting in the Lord and do what is right in His eyes. Fix your heart on the promises of God and you will be secure, feasting on His faithfulness. Make God the utmost delight and pleasure of your life, and He will provide for you what you desire the most. Give God *the right to direct your life*, and as you trust Him

along the way you'll find He pulled it off perfectly (Ps. 37:4–5 The Passion Translation,
emphasis added)!

Also, King Solomon offers wisdom:

Trust in the LORD with all your heart, and lean
not on your own understanding; In all your
ways acknowledge Him, and *He shall direct
your paths* (Prov. 3:5–6, emphasis added).

You see, you *can* trust Him to lead you in His ways. The
Holy Spirit will teach you, and everything will work out perfectly as you yield to His instruction and guidance.

CLEAVE TO HIM

The last prerequisite for "Heaven on Earth" is cleaving to
Him. The word "cleave" here means to adhere or attach, and
can also mean pursue. This definition indicates greater passion is involved in "cleaving to Him" than a lot of people have
heard or been taught. God loves to be pursued! I am well
aware that angels take note and relay information to Heaven
of our activity and words. I make sure the angels have good

reports to take back with them. You can, too. Pursue God! It is an "attention getter" in Heaven.

We need to abandon our own understanding about life and its difficulties and run to Him. Pursue Him and attach yourself to Him. He will take you where you need to go! Refuse to let go of Him until you get to your Heaven on Earth!

THE RESULTS: THEN THE LORD WILL!

I am encouraged by what the passage in Deuteronomy tells us happens when we adhere to all the prerequisites listed. I have seen the Lord move into and take over my realm. The Lord says that He will drive out the enemy and we will take land from them! Hallelujah! The Lord says the enemy will fear you and the blessings of the Lord will be yours. Days of Heaven on earth are here.

Even the soles of your feet shall claim land for God as Heaven comes to earth. You will find yourself walking in the authority of Jesus. No enemy will be able to stand before you as you love the Lord, walk in His ways and cleave to Him!

CHAPTER 2

The Personality of Jesus

J esus is amazing! When Heaven comes to earth, Jesus will be in the middle of it all. He loves to show up and get things moving. Where two or more are gathered in His name, there He is! In the midst (see Matthew 18:20)!

I would like to discuss the personality of Jesus. I have many experiences to share and I would love to give insight into the Word of God as well on the subject. If we want Heaven on Earth, we will be encountering a change in us as the atmosphere around us changes in His presence. Jesus has the ability to influence you to the point of a personality overhaul. Let's just say that *the real you* will come forward and be dominant when Jesus is near. Jesus does not hold back on where He stands on anything. He loves to stir things. The end result is healing, deliverance and worship! He loves to worship and He loves being worshipped! I want to look into some of the attributes of Jesus in 1 Corinthians 13:4-8 AMP:

Love endures long and is patient and kind; love never is envious nor boils over with jealousy, is not boastful or vainglorious, does not display itself haughtily. It is not conceited (arrogant and inflated with pride); it is not rude (unmannerly) and does not act unbecomingly. Love (God's love in us) does not insist on its own rights or its own way, for it is not self-seeking; it is not touchy or fretful or resentful; it takes no account of the evil done to it [it pays no attention to a suffered wrong]. It does not rejoice at injustice and unrighteousness, but rejoices when right and truth prevail. Love bears up under anything and everything that comes, is ever ready to believe the best of every person, its hopes are fadeless under all circumstances, and it endures everything [without weakening]. Love never fails [never fades out or becomes obsolete or comes to an end].

Additionally, I would like to expound on similar lists of Holy Spirit influenced personality traits found in Galatians 5:22-23 and Ephesians 5:9:

But the fruit of the Spirit is love, joy, peace, longsuffering, kindness, goodness, faithfulness, gentleness, self-control.

For the fruit of the Spirit is in all goodness, righteousness, and truth.

HE ENDURES LONG

When Jesus is committed to someone, He has incomprehensible longevity to remain in the circumstance. Consider how He suffered greatly for us on the Cross, yet, during that suffering He maintained His position, to ensure complete propitiation of punishment for our sin. I have heard Jesus describe the suffering that He endured for us. His love amazes me and exceeds my comprehension; His great love allowed and strengthened Him to *endure such pain and hardship* for us.

HE IS PATIENT

We must accept that we are imperfect unlike Jesus, Who is without sin. We will never be good enough on our own. I was enthralled with His patience for me during my visitations. He understood my inability to comprehend certain truths. He remembers without Him, we are mere men, which is why He spends so much time teaching us through the Holy Spirit. He wants us to live in the truth (reality). When we fail, He is patient with us and understands our weaknesses because He lived in a body as well.

HE IS KIND

What can I say? He is the kindest person I have ever met. This is one of the main reasons why I did not want to come back to my life on earth. Why would you want to be away from the kindest person in the universe? Do not get me wrong, He is very direct, but kind at the same time.

HE IS SELFLESS

Every time I have encountered Jesus, He was thinking about me! When He asked me to do something for Him, it was ultimately for someone else. He takes care of His people. He doesn't need anything. He desires to give you what He has.

HE LOVES JUSTICE

I have seen Him address situations that needed justice. *HE WILL MAKE IT RIGHT ON YOUR BEHALF.* Just do not hinder Him; purpose to walk in forgiveness with everyone, and justice will come swiftly. He has a very large Law enforcement department (angels) at His disposal and they are well armed. Also, Jesus knows and has influence with the Judge. His Father is the Head Judge of the Universe!

HE LOVES TRUTH

The Word says that the truth will set you free (see John 8:23). When Jesus speaks, it is always the truth. He loves to see people get free and worship. He smiles when He sees truth reign because that was His Mission on the earth. He was sent to tell the truth about the Father and His Kingdom and set people free! Remember, HE SAW SATAN FALL LIKE LIGHTNING (see Luke 10:18)!

HE IS COMPASSIONATE

Many times Jesus had compassion on the people and healed them. He always wants to help. I know that we do not know what to do in some situations and we cry out to Him and He hears us. Other times we are silent and He still hears us and answers us. We are dear to Him.

HE LOVES RIGHTEOUSNESS

He loves the righteous ways of the Father. Everything in the universe was set in righteousness. Now, through the mighty work of salvation, Jesus is waiting for this world's kingdoms to become the Kingdoms of His Father, our God. He will reign as King over all the earth (see Revelation 11:16).

HE BEARS UP UNDER ANYTHING

The Lord has proven that He can bear the sins of the world. I know that He can bear your burden also.

Casting all your care upon Him, for He cares for you (1 Peter 5:7).

"Take My yoke upon you and learn from Me, for I am gentle and lowly in heart, and you will find rest for your souls. For My yoke is easy and My burden is light" (Matthew 11:29–30).

HE BELIEVES THE BEST

The time I spent with Jesus made me know that not only does He want the best for me, but He also *believes the best of me*. Very few people understand this. He is *for you* and He does not doubt you. I'm telling you this because if you get this, you will be *set free*!

HE WANTS THE BEST FOR EVERYONE

Jesus is looking for faith. As soon as He finds faith, He answers it. When we discern who He is and what He has done for us, we begin to speak and act out His intentions. At this point, all of Heaven jumps in and you will begin to have Days of Heaven on Earth. Amen.

HE IS HUMBLE

Being humble does not mean you are weak. I have never once thought that Jesus was weak. He is very strong but very wise. He will let you do what you want if you choose and find out the hard way, or you can ask for His help, and it will come quickly. I always ask now, and life is getting easier for me. How about you? Being humble is being wise.

HE IS CONFIDENT

Being confident in Him is not being prideful; it is called submission. Also, being confident in Him is humility! Jesus always does the will of the Father and *that* brings confidence!

HE PAYS NO ATTENTION TO A SUFFERED WRONG

Jesus has seen it all, and yet He still asks, "What can I do for you? My plans for you are awesome!" He asked the Father to forgive those who crucified Him (see Luke 23:34)! Repent and let it go, my friend! Your miracle is coming.

HE IS GOOD

Or do you despise the riches of His goodness, forbearance, and longsuffering, not knowing that the goodness of God leads you to repentance (Romans 2:3–4)?

Every time I have had a visitation with Him, I end up repenting. He is that good!

HE IS FAITHFUL

He truly is a friend that sticks closer than a brother. Even when we are faithless, He is still faithful because that is Who He is all the time. He is always there for His own.

HE IS GENTLE

Gentleness is not weakness. He brings peace and trust because He is so gentle. When the Spirit is moving, I sense the gentleness of Jesus leading me.

HE IS SELF-CONTROLLED

Jesus can teach us a thing or two about self-control. One of us has to have it all together at all times. We are not to let ourselves be distracted by the flesh or evil spirits.

HE IS HOLY

I have encountered this trait to the max with Him and felt blessed that I was able to be alive afterwards. There is no one like Him! There are no words for this one. Better to encounter it for yourself than me try to describe Him in this trait. He is Holy! Period! (see my Book *Heavenly Visitation.*)

HE IS BOLD

He can suddenly become as bold as a lion after being as gentle as a dove!

When you spend time around Jesus as the Days of Heaven come to the Earth, you will realize that you need massive amounts of healing and deliverance. Once you have acknowledged this, you are going to receive. Jesus will work you over good and send you out whole and ready to do it for others. Get ready! The ministry of Jesus is coming forth!

HE IS A MIGHTY WARRIOR

The Lord will go forth like a mighty man, He will rouse up His zealous indignation and vengeance like a warrior; He will cry, yes, He will shout aloud, He will do mightily against His enemies (Isaiah 42:13 AMP).

I remember the time that the Lord visited me in a very unique manner. He had just asked me to talk to a friend about something that did not go over as well as I thought. It was an uncomfortable situation, even though I had been completely obedient to the Lord by talking to him. I was distraught about the situation because I wanted everything to work out between us. I wanted the Lord to help me with some of my relationships that were hurting because people did not want to keep moving in step with the Lord and His plan. I prepared to go on a run and left for the path as usual. I ran this path almost daily. As I settled into my pace, I noticed that the presence of the Lord increased suddenly. My view of the desert in Arizona mysteriously disappeared on my left as Jesus came to speak with me on the path. I had the complete encounter with Him without breaking my stride! Suddenly, I could not see my surroundings, but could hear my running steps just the same. He was magnificent looking. He had long, flowing hair, and was dressed in an immaculate warrior garment made of very high quality material with a two-piece tunic (blue over red) with a gold breastplate on top of it. He wore accessories, such as forearm guards, a belt, shin guards and other ornamentation. Some accessories were pure gold, and, of course, a sword was sheathed at His side. As He approached me, I was taken away with Him to a place where we stood and talked for several minutes. I forgot about my life on earth as I had in 1992 when I died and spent 45 minutes with Him.

He was so handsome and brave as He stood there ready to go to battle! He is mighty in battle and no one can stand before Him! When He stands beside you, no one can stand before you to harm you either!

He said to me, "Kevin, because you have taken a stand for me, I am taking a stand for you!" He then reached to

His side and pulled out the most amazing sword that I have ever seen, gold with many beautiful jewels on the handle. He turned and walked away; going forth to fight my battles drawn sword in hand. I immediately was placed back on the running path without missing a stride, weeping for the next mile or so as I ran. He is a warrior.

CHAPTER 3

Your Relationship with Him

Let's look at our relationship with the Lord Jesus. I want to encourage you to know Him better. In any relationship, there must be a bond of trust developed between two people. I sense that at times, Jesus knew I was not ready for certain things that I had thought should happen in my life. I realize now that when I matured to a desired level, I could handle a lot more than previously. He then revealed to me more of Him and gave me the desires of my heart.

As your understanding of the realm of God's Kingdom increases, so will your participation in that realm. As you develop your faith, your area of operation in the realms of God (the Kingdom) will expand and you will have more entrusted to you from the Lord.

BEING HONEST

I would like to discuss a subject that is vital to a relationship: honesty. Three areas where honesty must be found are: in your heart, in your mind and in your relationships with God and others.

The Gospel of Luke tells us that an honest and good heart is good ground for the Word of God to be sown:

> But that on the good ground are they, which in an honest and good heart, having heard the word, keep it, and bring forth fruit with patience (Luke 8:15 KJV).

The Apostle Paul, addressing the Corinthians, said that honesty was important in the sight of God as well as each other:

> Avoiding this, that no man should blame us in this abundance which is administered by us: *Providing for honest things*, not only in the sight of the Lord, but also in the sight of men (2 Corinthians 8: 20–21, emphasis added KJV).

Paul also felt it important to tell the Philippians that there were things which they should dwell on in their thoughts, one of them being "honest things":

> Finally, brethren, whatsoever things are true, *whatsoever things are honest*, whatsoever things are just, whatsoever things are pure, whatsoever things are lovely, whatsoever things are of good report; if there be any virtue, and if there be any praise, think on these things (Phil. 4:8 KJV, emphasis added).

A Key to your relationship thriving with Jesus is to mature to the place of implementation into His Kingdom activities. You become a co-laborer with Jesus in the Kingdom business. The Trinity has big plans for every person on the earth whether they know it or not.

As you may have heard me say here and in previous works, the Holy Spirit is referred to as the Spirit of Truth by Jesus (see John 14:17). The word "truth" in a Greek word study yields the definition "reality". The Amplified Bible depicts this accurately:

A time will come, however, indeed it is already here, when the true (genuine) worshipers will worship the Father in spirit and in *truth (reality)*; for the Father is seeking just such people as these as His worshipers (John 4:23, emphasis added).

I mention all of this for a reason. When Heaven comes to the earth, the Spirit of Truth will manifest. The Spirit will manifest "reality" and will permeate your world and your very being and demand some changes. This will require you to yield to the truth or "reality." A good and honest heart is a perfect place for the Word of God to spring forth. If you have an open and honest relationship with the Lord, knowing that He sees and knows everything, you can yield and reconcile with Him and let the process of correction proceed because you are being honest and willing to change. Remember, the Trinity doesn't need to change—we do. So be honest and let your world get rocked with a dose of Heavenly reality as Heaven visits the earth.

The Holy Spirit is within us and upon us to lead us into all "reality." As we yield ourselves in honesty with the Lord, we experience correction. After

the process is finished, we are taken into Days of
Heaven on Earth.

BEING TRANSPARENT

The Lord God seems to favor certain architecture. As you read and study the Bible, you will notice certain things mentioned more often than others. Transparency is one such item. Let's look at Revelation 4:6:

> And in front of the throne there was also what looked like a *transparent glassy sea*, as if of crystal. And around the throne, in the center at each side of the throne, were four living creatures (beings) who were full of eyes in front and behind [with intelligence as to what is before and at the rear of them] (emphasis added).

In Revelation 21:18 we read, "The wall was built of jasper, while the city [itself was of] pure gold, clear and *transparent like glass*" (emphasis added).

As you may know, there are parallels in the spiritual and physical realms. The author of Hebrews refers to these parallels as a "copy and shadow" of Heavenly things (see Hebrews 8:5). When Jesus speaks, there are multiple levels to everything He says. When I was with Him in 1992 (see my book *Heavenly Visitation*), I discerned something about Jesus's personality that has changed my life. Jesus wants us to be transparent. I was made aware of how He already knows everything about you—even your very thoughts. This did not embarrass me as much as it humbled me. I realized that yielding to Truth (reality) is a shortcut to my success. There are shortcuts, and transparency is one. You can accept what I just told you and expedite the maturity process, or you will continue on your current path and hinder your maturity process. The author of the book of Hebrews confirms this:

> Let us labour therefore to enter into that rest, lest any man fall after the same example of unbelief. For the Word of God is quick, and powerful, and sharper than any two-edged sword, piercing even to the dividing asunder of soul and spirit, and of the joints and marrow, and is a discerner of the thoughts and intents of the heart. Neither is there any creature that is not manifest in his sight: but all things are naked and opened unto the eyes of him with whom we have to do. Seeing then that we have a great high priest, that is passed into the Heavens,

Jesus the Son of God, let us hold fast our pro-
fession. For we have not a high priest which
cannot be touched with the feeling of our infirmities; but was in all points tempted like as
we are, yet without sin. Let us therefore come
boldly unto the throne of grace that we may
obtain mercy, and find grace to help in time of
need (Hebrews 4:11–16 KJV, emphasis added).

*By permitting the Spirit of Reality to permeate us, we
enable His holy presence to reveal the true meaning
of our lives. Confess your sins (shortcomings) and
yield to what God has written about you in Heaven.
Be transparent before Him and allow Him to lead
and guide you. He loves you so very much. Big things
are in store for those who trust in Him.*

KNOWING WHERE YOU END AND HE BEGINS

The Holy Spirit has said this many times through me to
people, "Do not allow your heart to be troubled; impossible
situations prepare you for the supernatural. My power is
surely made manifest through your weakness."

One of the quickest ways to come into God's power is
through weakness. The apostle Paul writes:

And He said to me, "My grace is sufficient for you, for My strength is made perfect in [your] weakness." Therefore most gladly I will rather boast in my infirmities, that the power of Christ may rest upon me (2 Corinthians 12:9, emphasis added).

Also Paul emphasizes dying to the flesh and the life of Christ living in Believers through resurrection:

I have been crucified with Christ; it is no longer I who live, but Christ lives in me; and the life which I now live in the flesh I live by faith in the Son of God, Who loved me and gave Himself for me (Galatians 2:20).

We need to understand where we end and He begins. This wisdom comes from Heaven. Most people do not understand the parameters in our spiritual walk with God and are unaware of what is happening in the spiritual realm all around them. Your spirit can be trained to be "situationally aware." Pilots are trained in this. I understand "situational awareness" because it was engrained in me during my years of pilot training. Being situationally aware is necessary to being a good pilot. Pilots continually assess their conditions;

looking ahead to where they are traveling, monitoring systems on the airplane as well as their position at any moment. Operating in the spiritual realm is very similar. You have the Word of God as your maps and your manuals; and as a Christian, you have the Spirit of God as your internal guidance system to lead you along your destined path.

Another important trait of a good pilot is recognizing and acknowledging any limitations, not only your own as a human, but also the equipment that you fly. I know when I feel overloaded that I need to ask for assistance, but the airplane doesn't have that ability. That is why its manual lists the plane's previously determined limitations. The plane is sent to a test facility where engineers subject the craft to simulated situations exceeding the plane's structural capability, as well as strenuously testing the airplane's other systems. When the airplane is thoroughly tested in all aspects, the limitations for the airplane are published and a pilot is not to exceed them. Christians have been given the Word of God as our operating manual. Spiritually, the limitations are removed, because Jesus said all things are possible to those who believe. Physically, it is a different story. Unless the spiritual intervenes in our physical life, our bodies will decay because of the condition of fallen man. Human life expectancy was 1000 years immediately after the fall. We went from living forever to living 1000 years because of the effects of sin. Now contemporary life expectancy is around 80 years, yet there is more revelation of the Word of God today than there has ever been. Realizing that we have limitations when separated from supernatural intervention is integral for properly "assessing your condition." With Holy Spirit's guidance, you can have spiritual situational awareness.

Paul said that when he was weak, he was strong, because in weakness the power of God was revealed. The supernatural is activated when God intervenes in our "natural." Because He is above the natural, anything He does to our natural is supernatural. Part of the wisdom that Jesus gave me was to know where I end and where He begins. Once these lines are defined for you, you will live in the supernatural all the time. You see, it's not about us, it's about Him. We have been bought with a price, and the life we live in the flesh we ought no longer to live for ourselves (1 Corinthians 6:19). The more quickly you accept this and crucify your flesh, the more quickly you will experience the resurrection and live in power. Part of the wisdom received from Jesus is allowing Him to define where you end and where He begins. This sacred work is necessary for the supernatural to operate. Sadly, most people never experience what I have described, and thusly, never experience the supernatural that God intends to happen. Forbid others' ignorance

from hindering you. Step out and begin to participate in the
Days of Heaven on Earth.

> *As you discern and acknowledge your limitations*
> *also know that God stands at that line where your*
> *ability ends, waiting to take you over into the super-*
> *natural! So, yield to the supernatural and allow Him*
> *to carry you across the barrier of where you end and*
> *He begins! Enjoy your journey. This is your appointed*
> *time to step through!*

ACCEPTING FORGIVENESS

Another helpful tool in your relationship with Jesus is
the essential ability to accept His forgiveness. We all know
that we are not perfect. We have all been told that there is
forgiveness when you confess your sin. He is faithful and
just to forgive you and cleanse you from all unrighteousness
(see 1 John 1:9). A necessary step in your walk with Jesus
is recognizing that when He died on the cross, He bought
you completely—forever. Not just for certain sins or certain
times and dispensations of your life. The truth of it is that
the cross took care of future trespasses as well! As long as
you walk humbly before Him and do not take advantage of
the fact that you're already forgiven—you are forgiven! I'm

not talking about apathy to sin, "I can go on sinning, I'm for-given." No! I'm talking about people need to accept the for-giveness that Jesus gave when He gave His life and bought you. He took care of the future so you can reconcile with God through confession of any sin that is outstanding between Him and you. Allow yourself to be cleansed from all unrigh-teousness. One of the most amazing things about Jesus is this: He means what He says! Hear Him now. He is saying to you, "I forgive you and your record is clean." Let the Holy Spirit speak right now as the truth permeates your heart. Not only are you forgiven but the record does not exist.

Jesus asks you to accept His forgiveness and allow Him to cleanse you from a guilty conscious. If He says, "your sins are forgiven," then they are! Getting this right is so important. He sees your relationship with Him as so important that He actually died for you. He loves you! Let the healing flow now as you sense His forgiveness take effect.

YIELDING

We must yield!

We have to realize that our responsibility down here on the earth is to yield to God. The Father is never going to get any more powerful, anymore able than He is right at this moment. Jesus is not going to get any more active on what He Has done for the Church.

It is finished! Jesus is seated at the right hand of God and the Holy Spirit has been sent with power to the Church (see Acts 1:8). Jesus is not going to get any more powerful, any holier, than He is right now. The Lord is ever present and His Spirit has been dispensed. Heaven has come to the earth! It's more about yielding because the change begins with us. The Word clearly says that God will not change (see Malachi 3:6), so why do we wait? If the change needs to begin in us, then let's yield and see God manifest.

Yielding has to do with our heart, it has to do with our faith, and it has to do with our willingness to walk away from ourselves and what we want. Then we do what He wants; which has a far greater reward.

HOLY CLEANSING FIRE

I remember right before September 11, 2001, the Lord Jesus appeared to me and ministered to me about His holy cleansing fire. As in all of His appearances to me, there was nothing on my part that triggered the visit. I had been involved in a church in Phoenix, Arizona where my wife and I attended. At the time, I was being groomed for full time ministry in their national organization. As we worshipped in the service Sunday morning, I opened my eyes to see the worship leader and the choir worshipping the Lord. To my surprise, off to my right was Jesus, standing beside the choir with His arms out in a receiving position, taking in our worship. You should have seen His face. He was in ecstasy as what we were doing pleased Him to the point of complete satisfaction!

I stopped and stared, because He was so beautiful to watch. He looked to be average height (just under six feet tall), with tanned skin and long brown hair with blonde highlights, which he parted down the middle. All of the sudden, He opened His eyes and knew that I was staring at Him. He had ignited with a bright flame and was burning freely in front of everyone. At this point I looked at the faces of all the people in the congregation to see their reaction to His appearance on the platform. Even my wife, who was beside me, did not see Him. I turned my attention back to the platform to behold the Master still burning; He was completely engulfed in flames from head to toe. I saw His right arm extend as He pointed directly at me! I noticed that a flaming stream was moving like lava away from Him and making its way off the platform and down the aisle toward me. My eyes had been opened by the Spirit and I had all my faculties. He was just as clear to me as all the people around Him.

Soon, the flaming lava reached my feet and started up my legs. This felt so clean. It was amazing! It was His cleansing fire. I felt healing as it moved up to consume me. The whole time, I was hoping others could see the Lord Jesus in this most special appearance.

I was excited, because at this point, I realized I was about to get what Jesus had. The flames were about to be all over me. I was being set aflame in Jesus name!

Then I became alarmed. As the flames passed my waist, I began to experience extreme pain. The flames proceeded up through my chest area, and the pain became excruciating. I stopped worshiping and put my arms down and looked at Jesus with that look that asks, "What in the world is going on?" Immediately, without saying a word, Jesus showed me His mission (intention).

I understood something about myself, as I burned. The area that the flames reached and were causing the pain was the area of my soul (mind, will and emotions)!

I experienced trouble breathing and I knew if things did not change, I would be in danger. When I looked back at Jesus, His face got a very stern look on it as He spoke to me out loud. With a roar He proclaimed, "Yield to the fire!" When He said that, everything shook. I made an internal adjustment and the pain suddenly stopped. The flames immediately went up over me and finished the cleansing work in me.

I realized afterward why I had gone through so many trials with so many people and situations in my life: I was being cleansed with Holy fire!

The fire burns today as I yield to what He is doing in my life. The flames won't extinguish because they are from Him. Yield to His Work. Do not fight the process any more. This world doesn't deserve you after you have been put through the fire and emerge pure. Pure gold without impurities! You are beautiful just like Him!

FAITH SPOKEN

Spending time with Jesus, as mentioned in my book *Heavenly Visitation*, profoundly changed my speech patterns. We need to cultivate our hearts by feeding on the Word of God, and when faith begins to sprout inside of us, we need to speak! Allow the Holy Spirit to ignite you with revelation and then you need to speak it! I have seen God act on my behalf in some of the most profound ways because I spoke my faith. Spoken faith activates the Holy Spirit, it activates angels, and it activates our authority against demonic spirits. Jesus told us to speak:

So Jesus answered and said to them, "Have faith in God. For assuredly, I say to you, whoever says to this mountain, 'Be removed and be cast into the sea,' and does not doubt in his heart, but believes that those things he says will be done, he will have whatever he says. Therefore I say to you, whatever things you ask when you pray, believe that you receive them, and you will have them" (Mark 11:22–24, emphasis added).

So speak out your faith! It is a part of your relationship with the Lord. He told us to speak to our mountains and we need to speak!

REALM OF INFLUENCE

Apostle John writes of his encounter with an angel in Revelation 19:9-10:

Then he said to me, "Write, 'Blessed are those who are called to the marriage supper of the Lamb!'" He continued, "These are the true sayings of God." I fell at his feet to worship him. But he said to me, "See that you do not do that! I am your fellow servant, and of your brethren who

have the testimony of Jesus. Worship God! For
the testimony of Jesus is the Spirit of Prophecy."

We need to testify about Jesus as much as possible. The
book of Revelation clearly indicates the testimony of Jesus
is the Spirit of Prophecy. I have witnessed some of the most
profound visitations after I began to talk about Jesus to the
unsaved: the unbeliever. The whole room fills up with angels
and the presence of God. I feel as though I am participating
in the powers of the coming age (see Hebrews 6:4, 5). Make
sure you have a good, well-planned testimony for delivery.
Also, make sure that you're always ready to testify—in
season and out of season—by the Spirit!

Testifying strengthens your relationship with Jesus and
you will sense Him ever so near when you speak of Him. I
know that there have been instances when He was in the
room while I was testifying about Him. He was smiling!

Remember, testifying about Him is the Spirit of Prophecy.

CHAPTER 4

When Heaven Arrives: Holy Spirit, Glory, and Angels

N ext, I want to portray about what happens when Heaven arrives on the earth. I know that the Kingdom of God originated in Heaven. Heaven is a timeless realm that has always existed. Because it is in a different dimension than the earth, Heaven is not limited by distance. When this supernatural Kingdom comes in contact with the earth, anything that is not in line with the Kingdom will have to get out of the way or change. The Holy Spirit will convict the world of sin, righteousness, and judgment as part of this process:

> Nevertheless I tell you the truth. It is to your advantage that I go away; for if I do not go away, the Helper will not come to you; but if I depart, I will send Him to you. And when He has come,

He will convict the world of sin, and of righteousness, and of judgment: of sin, because they do
not believe in Me; of righteousness, because I go
to My Father and you see Me no more; of judgment, because the ruler of this world is judged
(John 16:7–11).

The Kingdom of God is the Government of Heaven. When
the Government of Heaven comes to earth, you will see
change. When you yield to this Kingdom, the Holy Spirit will
begin to reveal truth and conviction will come. Angel activity
will increase as well because angels are the military branch
of the Kingdom. God's glory will arrive when there is submission and divine order in place.

HOLY SPIRIT

The Holy Spirit was poured out on the day of Pentecost.
Since that day, the Church has grown to cover the earth
with believers. The Holy Spirit is the life of the true Church.
Remember, the Lord has appointed seasons for everything
and we are entering into the Days of Heaven on Earth.
Let's look at what happened at the birth of the Church as
we know it:

He said to them, It is not for you to become acquainted with and know what time brings [the things and events of time and their definite periods] or fixed years and seasons (their critical niche in time), which the Father has appointed (fixed and reserved) by His own choice and authority and personal power. But you shall receive power (ability, efficiency, and might) when the Holy Spirit has come upon you, and you shall be My witnesses in Jerusalem and all Judea and Samaria and to the ends (the very bounds) of the earth (Acts 1:7–8 AMP, emphasis added).

Jesus foretold of the day when He would leave earth. He promised He would not leave His people as orphans but would send to them the Holy Spirit and they would become witnesses for Him. The Holy Spirit would remind them of what Jesus had spoken and would tell them the future as well.

But the Comforter (Counselor, Helper, Intercessor, Advocate, Strengthener, Standby), the Holy Spirit, Whom the Father will send in My name [in My place, to represent Me and act on My behalf], He will teach you all things. And

He will cause you to recall (will remind you of, bring to your remembrance) everything I have told you (John 14:26 AMP, emphasis added).

But when He, the Spirit of Truth (the Truth-giving Spirit) comes, He will guide you into all the Truth (the whole, full Truth). For He will not speak His own message [on His own authority]; but He will tell whatever He hears [from the Father; He will give the message that has been given to Him], and He will announce and declare to you the things that are to come [that will happen in the future] (John 16:13 AMP).

The Holy Spirit came. We enjoy the outpouring and the manifestations that followed including speaking in tongues, miracles, signs and wonders, and fruits and gifts of the Spirit. The Spirit of God comes and manifests; it's that simple. Paul describes the gifts of the Spirit. He writes in First Corinthians that the Spirit gives us gifts as He wills:

NOW ABOUT the spiritual gifts (the special endowments of supernatural energy), brethren, I do not want you to be misinformed.

You know that when you were heathen, you were led off after idols that could not speak [habitually] as impulse directed and whenever the occasion might arise. Therefore I want you to understand that no one speaking under the power and influence of the [Holy] Spirit of God can [ever] say, Jesus be cursed! And no one can [really] say, Jesus is [my] Lord, except by and under the power and influence of the Holy Spirit: Now there are distinctive varieties and distributions of endowments (gifts, extraordinary powers distinguishing certain Christians, due to the power of divine grace operating in their souls by the Holy Spirit) and they vary, but the [Holy] Spirit remains the same. And there are distinctive varieties of service and ministration, but it is the same Lord [Who is served]. And there are distinctive varieties of operation [of working to accomplish things], but it is the same God Who inspires and energizes them all in all. But to each one is given the manifestation of the [Holy] Spirit [the evidence, the spiritual illumination of the Spirit] for good and profit. To one is given in and through the [Holy] Spirit [the power to speak] a message of wisdom, and to another [the power to express] a word of knowledge and understanding according to the same [Holy] Spirit; To another [wonder-working] faith by the same [Holy] Spirit, to another the extraordinary powers of healing by the one Spirit; To another the working of miracles, to another prophetic insight (the gift of interpreting the divine will and purpose); to another the ability to discern and distinguish between [the utterances of true] spirits [and false ones], to another various kinds of [unknown] tongues, to another the ability to interpret [such] tongues. All these [gifts, achievements, abilities] are inspired and brought to pass by one and the same [Holy] Spirit, Who apportions to each person individually [exactly] as He chooses (1 Corinthians 12:1–11 AMP, emphasis added).

Also, Paul mentions the fruit of the Spirit in the book of Galatians. We have the opportunity to manifest these wonderful characteristics of Heaven in our lives. We need to yield to the Holy Spirit.

But the fruit of the [Holy] Spirit [the work which His presence within accomplishes] is love, joy (gladness), peace, patience (an even temper, forbearance), kindness, goodness (benevolence), faithfulness, Gentleness (meekness, humility), self-control (self-restraint, continence). Against such things there is no law [that can bring a charge]. And those who belong to Christ Jesus (the Messiah) have crucified the flesh (the godless human nature) with its passions and appetites and desires. If we live by the [Holy] Spirit, let us also walk by the Spirit [If by the Holy Spirit we have our life in God, let us go forward walking in line, our conduct controlled by the Spirit.] (Galatians 5:22–25 AMP).

We also have enjoyed the gifts and callings of God in people which include the "fivefold ministry" as listed in Ephesians:

He is the one who gave these gifts to the Church: the apostles, the prophets, the evangelists, and the pastors and teachers. Their responsibility is to equip God's people to do his work and build up the Church, the body of Christ, until we come to such unity in our faith and knowledge of God's Son that we will be mature and full grown in the Lord, measuring up to the full stature of Christ (Ephesians 4:11–13 NLT, emphasis added).

These gifts represent the Kingdom of God as the Spirit of God moves people to manifest "Kingdom Government" by the Holy Spirit. The Holy Spirit causes Heaven to come and bring structure to earth. As long as man does not interfere and try to control the Holy Spirit, the Church will be alive and function in power. If man tries to control the Heavenly Government, he will grieve the Holy Spirit and the Spirit will not manifest but will pullback. We must not grieve the Holy Spirit. We must allow Him to advance and manifest.

The Holy Spirit is wonderful! He manifests the Government of Heaven!

GLORY

And He said, "My Presence will go with you, and I will give you rest." Then he said to Him, "If Your Presence does not go with us, do not bring us up from here. For how then will it be known that Your people and I have found grace in Your sight, except You go with us? So we shall be separate, Your people and I, from all the people who are upon the face of the earth." So the LORD said to Moses, "I will also do this thing that you have spoken; for you have found grace in My sight, and I know you by name." And he said, "Please, show me Your glory." Then He said, "I will make all My goodness pass before you, and I will proclaim the name of the LORD before you. I will be gracious to whom I will be gracious, and I will have compassion on whom I will have compassion." But He said, "You cannot see My face; for no man shall see Me, and live." And the LORD said, "Here is a place by Me, and you shall stand on the rock. So it shall be, while My glory passes by, that I will put you in the cleft of the rock, and will cover you with My hand while I pass by. Then I will take away My hand, and you shall see My back; but My face shall not be seen" (Exodus 33:14–23).

Glory is a mystery. I personally believe glory is another dimension of God, which He can veil or unveil. Some people misidentify God's glory as simply the Holy Spirit's presence, but it's more! When the glory is manifested we cannot look at His face. You see, God's presence was with Israel in the desert, but when we look at Moses and his account, we find that Moses had spent a lot of time face-to-face with God on the mountain. He asked God to come by and show Him His glory. Moses had been up there with Him during the giving of the law for extended periods of time. Now God said He would show him His Glory but not His face.

So glory must be stronger than presence. Moses was able to see some of the glory but not what was coming from the face of God. I think this is the key. Moses' face shone bright and had to be veiled because he had been in God's presence and the people were afraid. God in all His Glory would be much too strong if His face were exposed with Glory manifesting!

> ...Who being the brightness of His glory and the express image of His person, and upholding all things by the word of His power, when He had by Himself purged our sins, sat down at the right hand of the Majesty on high (Hebrews 1:3 NKJV, emphasis added).

Jesus is the Glory the came out of the Father. Jesus is the exact image of God the Father.

The name of God was then given by Moses to Aaron, the first high priest. The name was then transferred to each high priest throughout the years of the high priesthood. No one on the outside actually knows how to pronounce that name, it was only pronounced in the holy of holies once a year and it was done with blood being present. The glory was between the cherubim on the ark but the face of God was not seen there.

We are going to encounter the glory of God but I
believe that there will have to be some adjustments
made in the near future because He is holy and there
is only a certain degree a man can take.

I was not allowed to see Jesus's face when this glory was manifested (see my book *Heavenly Visitation* for a complete account). I have seen Jesus's face at times but the one time that the glory was manifested I was not able to look at His face. I felt that I would not live to tell about it if I did look.

Jesus wants us to know His Presence. If we want to see His Glory, it will be a part of Him that He unveils with discretion to those He chooses. The time is coming when we will see this splendor, His Glory!

ANGELS

And of the angels He says: "Who makes His angels spirits and His ministers a flame of fire."

But to which of the angels has He ever said: "Sit at My right hand, till I make Your enemies Your footstool"? Are they not all ministering spirits sent forth to minister for those who will inherit salvation (Hebrews 1:7, 13, 14)?

Angels are God's agents sent to serve for those who will *inherit salvation*. They only hearken to the word of the Lord, are flames of fire, and do the Lord's bidding. They have been assigned to orchestrate and maintain this move that has started. I was told that the angels were already here with their equipment and that the move was glorious. During a visitation, the angels told me not to wait to get into the move and they instructed me to carry the presence correctly, just as the Levites had to carry the Ark of the Covenant correctly under the old covenant. Heaven has come to the earth and the angels have a great deal to do with it. Angels have been sent to bring the believers up to speed. I was told that angels are sent at the end of the dispensation before another dispensation starts. When things lag, their activity increases in order to bring the people up to speed.

We see in the book of Daniel that angels are part of the "government of God" and they are here to help you fulfill everything you're called to do. They can help you to be more effective in ministry and there are a lot of them.

Yield to the government of God! The Holy Spirit is present, the glory is present, and the angels are present. Angels are operating and they will not accept "no" for an answer. They have been sent! They are waiting on you! We are not waiting on them.

The move has started and the angels are here!

CHAPTER 5

Phase One: Revelation

⁓

Next, Jesus wants me to share about the first phase, *Revelation*, to come during *Days of Heaven on Earth.* Paul discusses this in Ephesians chapter one. Let's look at that passage:

[For I always pray to] the God of our Lord Jesus Christ, the Father of glory, that He may grant you a spirit of wisdom and revelation [of insight into mysteries and secrets] in the [deep and intimate] knowledge of Him, By having the eyes of your heart flooded with light, so that you can know and understand the hope to which He has called you, and how rich is His glorious inheritance in the saints (His set-apart ones), And [so that you can know and understand] what is the immeasurable and unlimited and surpassing greatness of His power in and for us who believe, as demonstrated in the working of His mighty strength, Which He exerted in Christ when He raised Him from the dead and seated Him at His [own] right hand in the Heavenly [places], Far above all rule and authority and power and dominion and every name that is named [above every title that can be conferred], not only in this age and in this world, but also in the age and the world which are to come. And He has put all things under His feet and has appointed Him the universal and supreme Head of the Church [a headship exercised throughout the Church], [Psalms 8:6.] Which is His body, the fullness of Him Who fills all in all [for in that body lives the full measure of Him Who makes everything complete, and Who fills everything everywhere with Himself](Ephesians 1:17–23 AMP, emphasis added).

As you can see, the prayer that Paul prays allows the eyes of their heart to be enlightened. He goes step by step through the exciting things that God has for us. Revelation is coming to the Church.

PACKAGES FROM HEAVEN

1. HOPE—You can know and understand the hope to which He has called you.
2. INHERITANCE—How rich is His glorious inheritance in the saints (His set-apart ones).
3. POWER—What is the immeasurable and unlimited and surpassing greatness of His power in and for us who believe.
4. FAR ABOVE—Far above all rule and authority and power and dominion and every name that is named [above every title that can be conferred], not only in this age and in this world, but also in the age and the world which are to come.

This exciting phase will bring much healing and deliverance. Right now more revelation is being given by the Spirit of God to the Church than any other time. That doesn't mean that the increase was on God's part; revelation has always been available through the work of Jesus.

The fact is, people are praying these prayers in Ephesians for themselves and revelation is flowing! The Spirit is moving on a lot of people right now to speak from Heaven's perspective.

REVELATION PRODUCES INTIMACY

When Heaven comes to earth, the first thing that happens is the Spirit of God hovers over the Body of Christ, like He hovered over the face of the waters in the book of Genesis. Lately, there is kind of a vibration or brooding "in the Spirit" inside me and my wife when the Holy Spirit comes to us. This is affirmed in word studies:

The earth was without form and an empty waste, and darkness was upon the face of the very great deep. The Spirit of God was moving (*hovering, brooding*) over the face of the waters (Genesis 1:2 AMP Emphasis added).

At times your eyes are open and the Spirit of God will start to teach you and bring you into a place of intimacy in the knowledge of Him.

The apostle Paul was caught up and given the revelation of Jesus Christ. We have all of the epistles that were written by him. He was given this revelation by Jesus himself and not by any man. This is intimate and personal attention given through the Spirit of revelation.

Jesus spoke about the Holy Spirit coming and being the One who would reveal Him, remind the Church what He had said, as well as foretell future events. We see this in John's Book of Revelation; the Revelation of Jesus Christ. John sees future events and records them before they happen. That is revelation!

THE DEEP THINGS OF GOD

Be infused with the breath of Heaven and let revelation flow from God's heart to your heart now in the name of Jesus!

Yet to us God has unveiled and revealed them by and through His Spirit, for the [Holy] Spirit searches diligently, exploring and examining everything, even sounding the profound and bottomless things of God [the divine counsels and things hidden and beyond man's scrutiny] (1 Corinthians 2:10 AMP).

The Spirit of God has the ability to unveil truth to us. I would like to share one these nuggets of truth with you, shown to me through a wonderful time of a "deep unveiling" of Jesus's heart to me.

A PROFOUND REVELATION

In prayer I saw Jesus appear unexpectedly to speak at a church: He walks up and greets the crowd. Everyone is amazed that He is the "guest speaker" today. As He begins to introduce His plans for the people, church, community, and city, a man stands. It is a student named Peter. He stops Jesus and says, "Lord, it is good that You are here, let's build a place for You to abide." Then a lady named Martha stands, turns around and runs off to start cooking, yelling for Mary to help her instead of hearing what the Lord is about to tell them. A man, dominated by demons (even though He has been in the Church for years), stands and yells, "Son of God, have You come to torment us before our time?" Next, a rich young ruler gets up and walks out because he wanted to hear a motivational teaching on "success in Life," without it costing him anything in the process. Then, a board member named Pilate stands and yells, "What is truth?" He ends up leaving; upset because no one ran the "guest speaker" idea by him before the service. Judas, the Church treasurer comes up and kisses Jesus on the cheek then walks out. He is seen in the church parking lot calling 911. He tells the operator that the Church has been seized by a religious extremist and a SWAT team may be needed. He leaves his contact information with the police in order to collect any reward that might be offered. Jesus raises His hands to calm the people. Just then, two young men (James and John) stand and ask the Lord if they should call down fire from Heaven on all of them. With tears in His eyes, He asks the congregation, "I thought that My Father said that this is about Me and My Kingdom? When did it become about you and your kingdom? I have plans for this area and you're included!" The people chorus, **"Why, Lord, it is about You**!" Jesus continues, "If it's about Me, then why did I spend the night on a park bench last night; all of your doors were locked and no one took Me in and fed Me? And, last week, I was thrown in jail for preaching in a restricted part of the city and you did not come by for a visit. I was lonely and you did not invite Me to any of your functions. If you will make it about Me and My Kingdom; which includes the 'least of these,' I will make it about you to My Father in Heaven. I guarantee it."

> "...for I was hungry and you gave Me no food; I was thirsty and you gave Me no drink; I was a stranger and you did not take Me in, naked and you did not clothe Me, sick and in prison and you did not visit Me."

Then they also will answer Him, saying, "Lord, when did we see You hungry or thirsty or a stranger or naked or sick or in prison, and did not minister to You?" Then He will answer them, saying, "Assuredly, I say to you, inasmuch as you did not do it to one of the least of these, you did not do it to Me." And these will go away into everlasting punishment, but the righteous into eternal life (Matthew 25:42-46 NKJV).

HOW DEEP DO YOU WANT TO GO?

Be sure to yield to the Spirit in times of prayer, fasting and separation; allowing your eyes and your ears to be open to what God is saying.

IN MANY separate revelations [each of which set forth a portion of the Truth] and in different ways God spoke of old to [our] forefathers in and by the prophets, [But] in the last of these days He has spoken to us in [the person of a] Son, Whom He appointed Heir and lawful Owner of all things, also by and through Whom He created the worlds and the reaches of space and the ages of time [He made, produced,

built, operated, and arranged them in order].
He is the sole expression of the glory of God
[the Light-being, the out-raying or radiance of
the divine], and He is the perfect imprint and
very image of [God's] nature, upholding and
maintaining and guiding and propelling the
universe by His mighty word of power. When
He had by offering Himself accomplished our
cleansing of sins and riddance of guilt, He sat
down at the right hand of the divine Majesty
on high, [Taking a place and rank by which] He
Himself became as much superior to angels as
the glorious Name (title) which He has inher-
ited is different from and more excellent than
theirs (Hebrews 1:1–4 AMP).

When I met Jesus, He wasn't like what some people
had portrayed Him as being. This is what He was like.
He said, "If you will listen to everything I say, and not
only hear it but see it as well, you will become 'the
answer.'" You will actually become the answer! You
will attract the answer. It will pursue you. There has
to be a change inside.

You must understand the time we are in and spiritual current events; now is the time to yield to the Holy Spirit. He wants to take you deeper. I need to yield more to what occurs around me in the Kingdom; I realize the Lord desires to do exceedingly more than I have planned. I want to emphasis that this is a supernatural time of "Heaven on Earth". In all likelihood, this was on the Lord's heart for us to know and experience a long time ago.

The Lord is saying to me that there are certain phases of what He has to accomplish that are not accomplished because of a lack of humility and complete yielding. I realized this when I was with Him. If you want to go deeper in God, then hang around Jesus. His personality will escort you to your destination quickly when you fully yield to Him. He is much more yielded to the Father than we are to Him (Jesus).

There's an element of Jesus's personality that is not being taught, preached or portrayed about Him. He is looking for you to breathe in what He says and not mentally ascend to it. In other words, do not just mentally agree and say, "Well, yeah, I believe that!" Act on what He says!

I AM THE DOOR

One early morning, while in my home in Seattle, I awoke and sat up in bed. There, at the foot of my bed, stood Jesus. He looked at me and said, "I am the Door." I looked at Him intently. He had said it as though I had never heard it before. I wondered, "Why does that happen a lot?" When He talks to me, He tells me things as though I have never heard it. I learned His reason is because I really did not "get it" yet. I said, "Lord, I know You are the Door; You said that in the book of John as you addressed Your disciples." He raised His arm and pointed His finger at me and said, "No, you do not understand. You do not go anywhere on this earth unless it's through Me!" Then He turned around and disappeared, walked out. I've had many visits that only last a short time. But in that short time, what He said has changed my life forever.

When He spoke, essentially He said, "Listen, the first phase of what is happening right now with the Church is the phase of revelation." He said, "The believers need to cry out and they need to pray the first chapter of Ephesians, starting with verses 17-23."

Ephesians 1:17-23 is Paul's prayer for the Church's eyes of their heart to be enlightened. The subject continues in Ephesians 3:14:

For this reason I bow my knees to the Father of our Lord Jesus Christ, from whom the whole family in Heaven and earth is named, that He would grant you, according to the riches of His glory, to be strengthened with might through His Spirit in the inner man, that Christ may dwell in your hearts through faith; that you, being rooted and grounded in love, may be able to comprehend with all the saints what is the width and length and depth and height—to know the love of Christ which passes knowledge; that you may be filled with all the fullness of God. Now to Him who is able to do exceedingly abundantly above all that we ask or think, according to the power that works in us, to Him be glory in the Church by Christ Jesus to all generations, forever and ever. Amen (Ephesians 3:14-21).

I realized that I was not praying for revelation. I was not praying that the eyes of my heart would be enlightened. I had been mentally bombarded with truth, but it stayed in the mental realm. Is that good? Revelation must be *spiritually discerned* for it to actually *take root and produce fruit.* I can hear and be emotionally moved by revelation, but if the revealed truth(s) do(es) not assimilate into my Spirit, I can walk away and forget them. When there's a true move of the Spirit of God - when God moves through a person, a song, an act of kindness, a cup of water, a smile - something penetrates inside of you, and you can feel a release similar to new life or growth. When God breathes, Life is released. Contrarily, someone might say something good yet their words are barren, despite its message being a good thing. But, Jesus promises *fruit that lasts* when we yield to Him (see John 15:16-17)!

THE THREE PHASES

Jesus showed me that revelation is a place where God's words to you become so real, that they create a place where you dwell. For example, I have seen in the Spirit God frame my world through revelation. I saw large beams built in my life from nothing because He spoke them. I saw a building being built for habitation; He wants to come and dwell. The first phase is the framing of the building *in revelation*. Then He'll eventually come *visit* you *in visitation*. Finally, He will come to live with you *in habitation*. See there are the three phases: revelation, visitation and habitation. He showed me that a lot of people – you'd be surprised at the percentage of people - never get past even the first phase.

I saw my life being framed by these beautiful, massive beams through what was revealed to me in the Word. The beams manifested as His Word became flesh in my life whether in a quiet time, a prayer time, or whether in the giving of a sandwich to the homeless person. Whatever His instruction, truth penetrated me and changed me internally while framing my world.

Just as the Lord repeated Himself to me, you may find He repeats Himself to you. You get like Peter – "Lord, You know that I love You." The repetition frustrated and upset Peter. But, you see, the Lord knew. He replied to Peter's declaration, "You say you're going to die with Me. But I tell you the truth, before the cock crows, you're going to deny me three times" (see Matthew26:34-35). The point I want to make is that we all have been in situations where we have mentally assented. We emotionally assessed our relationship, remaining in the soul realm rather than ascending to the Spiritual realm.

The bottom line is that Peter did not have a revelation that developed enough depth in him. When he was tested and tried, he was not able to carry out what he had vocalized. His love was no more than emotion; it was mental assent. Mental assent allows

you to agree with something but not take it to heart.
Revelation is heartfelt reality that bears fruit.

The difference between a temporal experience and a life changing experience is the presence of and the yielding to the Holy Spirit. Holy Spirit, or the Spirit of God, is not only a person, He is a *whole environment* in that He creates an environment wherever He goes. If you desire to create a spiritually catalytic environment, you must yield to Him. In order for the Holy Spirit to manifest fully, those in His presence must yield their vessels to Him. He has to be able to speak. He has to be able to lean so much onto you that He goes into you, and through you into the atmosphere.

I'm not talking about being "born again". This is a
step after the salvation experience (see Acts 19:1-
6). It's called walking with God! It's called being "in
the Spirit."

Jesus and the Holy Spirit can manifest today as they did in the Bible. Luke 5:17 tells us that Jesus was teaching, "And the power of the Lord was present to heal them." This verse depicts Jesus and "the power" in attendance as two separate entities. Jesus taught and the power of the Holy Spirit was there ready to heal. That speaks volumes to me, because you can be present, or physically near, but not really be "present," not having your whole heart engaged.

You can sign-in on a sheet of paper and say you were there, but were you really there? Did you participate? Did you yield? Did you even add to what was going on? Is there presence when you're present? The Holy Spirit can help you by being there with you.

REVELATION OF THE SPIRIT

What I found is that revelation is what the Holy Spirit does. But, it's also Who He is. He creates an environment; it's not just the Spirit of God showing up. It's Who He is. And if He leans on you, then all of a sudden you *see*, all of a sudden you *hear*. He gets so into you that you start to speak and you start to do. Before you know it, your environment becomes His environment. Then everybody in your sphere of influence starts to sense the same thing. They start hearing. They start seeing. They start doing.

Revelation can spread within a group of people as well. In Heaven, it is seen as a domino effect. The Holy Spirit leans on (influences) someone and they hear, see, and do. The repercussions of that event affect the environment around them and it begins to affect others in a similar fashion. Revelation becomes people's new reality. The group can become quite a threat to the enemy as they begin to take back territory, in prayer, for the "Ancient of Days".

Remember the Tower of Babel:

> And the Lord said, Behold, they are one people and they have all one language; and this is only the beginning of what they will do, and *now nothing they have imagined they can do will be impossible for them* (Genesis 11:6 AMP, emphasis added).

God had to come down and stop their plans. The Babylonians had one thing right: unity. They just had the wrong idea and called it "truth". We can see through this event that if we, as the body of Christ, will come into unity *even in our imagination*, nothing shall be impossible to us.

DISCIPLINE

The Spirit gives life. The flesh and the mind must be a servant to your inner man (your "born-again" spirit). Our flesh and mind have not been redeemed. Our mind needs to be renewed and our flesh needs to be subjected to discipline. Paul notes self-discipline:

But I *discipline* my body and bring it into subjection, lest, when I have preached to others, I myself should become disqualified (1 Corinthians 9:27, emphasis added).

He also writes in Romans 12:2:

And do not be conformed to this world, but be transformed by the *renewing of your mind*, that you may prove what is that good and acceptable and perfect will of God (emphasis added).

FRAMING MY WORLD

Remember the massive beams being built in my life? I saw that God was framing my world through revelation and that I was becoming a dwelling place for Him. I always wondered about the secret place of the Most High mentioned in Psalm 91. Studying the secret place created a deep longing to go to this place. I felt, "I've got to find the secret place, I've got to tuck myself into it, and then wait for God to show up and put His hand over my face so that I do not get torched when He passes!" (Let's address the glory of God again. As I mention throughout my writings, I have seen Jesus's face several times. But there was one time where I was not allowed to look at His face, and I always wondered, "Why?" I really felt I would die if I were to look up at His face at this point. [I did not understand the reason then. I expound on this in Chapter 7, *Phase Three: Habitation.*])

The secret place is a place of intimacy, where you and God can share secrets! Revelation is part of that process of building the secret place. Believe it or not, you are being prepared for the secret place. The Spirit of Truth is framing your house. When the Spirit has finished this phase in you, a beautiful structure will have been built for you and God to reside.

Paul implored God to dispense revelation on the Churches of Ephesus and Colossae. He prays for them in Chapters 1 and 3, respectively. Through His revelation to us, the Holy Spirit will show us Jesus. *His assignment is to reveal Jesus.* If a spirit isn't revealing Jesus, then it's not really the Spirit. If whatever is happening draws attention to something else, then it is not the Holy Spirit.

The Holy Spirit has been sent on a mission to convict the world of sin and righteousness. Conviction comes when Jesus is revealed, because *Jesus reflects God's goodness.* Romans 2:4 declare "the goodness of God leads you to repentance." Holy Spirit also reminds us of things Jesus said.

While my place is being built, the Holy Spirit coaches me and tells me Truth. He discloses, "Listen, this is what Jesus likes; this is what He likes to hear; this is what He likes you to do. If you do this, you will have favor."

The Holy Spirit is a master Builder and He is building us individually and corporately. We will become a habitation for Him:

> In Him [and in fellowship with one another] you yourselves also are being built up [into this structure] with the rest, to form a fixed abode (dwelling place) of God in *(by, through the Spirit)* (Ephesians 2:22-3:1 AMP, emphasis added).

DEAR KEVIN, WE ARE MOVING IN

When I do what the Spirit of God tells me to do; He takes me to a place where I have become a wonderful dwelling place for God. Our ultimate goal should be to fulfill what Jesus illustrates in John chapter 14:

> Jesus answered and said to him, "If anyone loves Me, he will keep *My word*; and My Father will

love him, and We will come to him and make Our home with him. He who does not love Me does not keep My words; and the word which you hear is not Mine but the Father's who sent Me" (John 14:23-24 NKJV, emphasis added).

"We will come to him and make Our home (abode, *special dwelling place*) with him" (John 14:23 AMP, emphasis added).

"My Father and I will come and live with you!" Wow! If you expand on those Scriptures through word studies, you will see how the words used are strong. They suggest that They are coming and bringing Their furniture with them to move in permanently. Permanent residence of the Trinity is our ultimate goal.

The Lord not only desires this for us individually, but also to have this for a group of people that know how to pray and intercede; that know how accomplish things through prayer. He wants to have a congregation who will not accept "no" for an answer about their city, their neighborhood or their mission focus. When you abide in the Spirit, and He in you, you pray yourself completely out of yourself and your concentration is not on your own needs. Correct priorities permit Heavenly provision – God will even pay your bills. He makes everything work out so much that now you are free to concentrate on your neighbor. Each church is designed to have several intercessors; you have people that know how to pray, but it's just a group of people. Even in the Old Testament, Moses longed for all of Israel (the whole congregation) to prophesy:

And Moses went out, and told the people the words of the LORD, and gathered the seventy men of the elders of the people, and set them round about the tabernacle. And the LORD came down in a cloud, and spake unto him, and took of the Spirit that was upon him, and gave it unto the seventy elders: and it came to pass, that, when the Spirit rested upon them, they prophesied, and did not cease. But there remained two of the men in the camp, the name of the one was Eldad, and the name of the other Medad: and the Spirit rested upon them; and they were of them that were written, but went not out unto the tabernacle: and they prophesied in the camp. And there ran a young man, and told Moses, and said, "Eldad and Medad do prophesy in the camp." And Joshua the son of Nun, the servant of Moses, one of his young men, answered and said, "My lord Moses, forbid them." And Moses said unto him, "Enviest thou for my sake? Would God that all the LORD's people were prophets, and that the LORD would put His Spirit upon them" (Numbers 11:24-29 KJV)!

Paul concurs in his writings, "I would that you all prophesy" (I Corinthians 14:5), and "Desire the spiritual gifts, especially prophecy, because it builds up the Church" (I Corinthians 14:1).

I'm not effective simply because Jesus appears to me; likewise, you're not effective just because Jesus speaks to you. What determines your effectiveness is *your response* to a Heavenly encounter – what you become, what happens to your environment, and what happens to your world around you. Transformation, while requiring effort, is not a chore. Transformation is about allowing Him to occupy your heart.

As conveyed already, revelation actually frames. The framework construction phase is vitally important. Sadly, mental ascension begets people parroting - they hear something and they just repeat it, without true revelation or Spiritual assimilation. I had a suspicion that even Peter was being checked by the Lord at times. He was being questioned because it seemed as though Jesus was trying to get some depth into him about what he was doing and saying.

That is what I feel He was doing with me, was that He was saying things to me and I was agreeing with Him because I had heard it and I could "parrot it"; I could actually repeat it like a parrot. But a parrot doesn't have a heartfelt passion about what he says; he doesn't even comprehend English. But to everyone, he sounds pretty intelligent, despite his not having any idea of his words' meaning. He is a parrot. You can train him to say something that is profound without him knowing his words' significance.

When I met the Lord, I realized my need for more correction than I thought I could handle. He was so gracious with me. I have discovered that if I do not depend upon the Spirit, if I do not allow Him to lean on me to the point where I allow Him to permeate me and I allow Him to give me new words, new ways, allowing the breath of God to breathe on me, then I do not have the tools to do anything more. I am unable to advance unless it's supernatural. I cannot force it, neither can you. Your Spirit-led walk will direct you to advance. The Holy Spirit will bring you to a point where you cannot go any further on your own and then you have to die. You recognize your need for Him to delve deeper into you, "Well, if I go any further, it's going to be supernatural." This phase of revelation is where you allow the Spirit to reveal another facet or layer of the Word of God. The result is your world framework is extended, that you become an even more spacious dwelling place for God. The beautiful framework appears as wood and is strong; because each beam is a pillar of Truth.

OIL FOR YOUR LAMP

Some of the profound revelations Jesus imparted to me during His appearances to me lasted just seconds. I am amazed how I could hear truth all my life and not know its true meaning and significance. When Jesus speaks Truth, He coaches you to receive His words in greater depth. He is pouring oil into your lamp. He is assisting you in storing oil for your future and destiny. He gently demonstrates, "You do not get it, because there's going to come a time where you're going to need this and you're not deep enough. You do not get it yet." When we listen, we can hear the Spirit of God speak Truth:

You really do not know how much I love you. What you are doing, you're doing for me, but you have no idea what it is accomplishing in the Spirit. So when

you do something, you're hoping that you're effec-
tive. The whole time, it is epic what you're doing. It's
sending out vibrations. It's shaping your environment
and it's affecting people around you.

He implores us that if we desire Him to visit us, we must yield to the Spirit of God and what He has given us already and visited us with the Word. Revelation comes from The Word. Jesus asked Peter, "Who do you say I am?" Peter answered, "You are the Christ, the Son of the living God." Jesus replied, "This was not revealed to you by man, but this was revealed to you by the Spirit." And upon this rock of revelation that Peter had just spoken, Jesus declared, "I am going to build My Church."

When I realized the Holy Spirit's intention to impart the personality of Jesus, I knew that the first several chapters of the book were to expound upon Jesus's nature, so we can discern His presence and activity. We must allow Him *to be Himself* in our lives. When we do not know His nature, then He has to actually step back until we recognize Him and yield to Him. Only then can we can represent Him and act like Him. I always wanted the ministry of Jesus, but I did not have the concept of that it's more about getting out of the way than it is about being a parrot. You're getting this, right?

CHAPTER 6

Phase Two: Visitation

⁄∿

J esus shared with me the 2nd phase of "*Days of Heaven on Earth*" is "*Visitation.*" This is when He comes and manifests in a special way and spends time but doesn't stay. As a friend Who visits, He may share intimate information (revelation) but does not stay permanently for any extended period of time. Of course we know He promises never to leave us or forsake us (Deuteronomy 31:6, John 14:18). I'm talking about in a relationship, you have times together and times apart. The Holy Spirit is with you always, but He may or may not manifest as strongly at times as in other special times.

God has plans for you, your family, your country, and the earth. Sometimes that involves paying a visit. If God has promised something, then because it is in His heart to fulfill that, He will perform it with whatever and with whomever it takes. Even if He has to come down Himself and do it:

> And Joseph said to his brethren, I am going to die. But God will surely *visit you and bring you out* of this land to the land He swore to Abraham, to Isaac, and to Jacob [to give you] (Genesis 50:24 AMP, emphasis added).

Also remember the conversation with Abraham:

> And the Lord said, *"Shall I hide from Abraham [My friend and servant] what I am going to do?"* (Galatians 3:8)

> ... And the Lord said, "Because the shriek [of the sins] of Sodom and Gomorrah is great and their sin is exceedingly grievous, I will go down now and see whether they have done altogether [as vilely and wickedly] as is the cry of it which has come to Me; and if not, I will know." Now the [two] men turned from there and went toward Sodom, but Abraham still stood before the Lord (Genesis 18:17, 20–22 AMP).

KINGDOM BUSINESS

Visitation involves Jesus or the Holy Spirit coming and manifesting in a supernatural way. This includes manifesting to the Church or its individual members at various times. The Holy Spirit will manifest with signs and wonders and miracles. Jesus Himself will come and be in the midst:

> "Again I say to you that if two of you agree on earth concerning anything that they ask, it will be done for them by My Father in heaven. For where two or three are gathered together in My name, *I am there in the midst of them*" (Matthew 18:19–20, emphasis added).

He is there in the midst! Visitation is Jesus interrupting the daily natural functions of life, which could be your workplace, recreation, sleep, or church gatherings. Jesus's presence increases the ability for people to enter into the supernatural (Please refer to my book *Heavenly Visitation* for teaching and accurate accounts of visitation).

INTIMATE DETAILS

During times of visitation, very private, intimate con-
versations can occur (see Genesis 18:17). I know that the
Lord, at any one moment, can share something with you
that would give you ultimate understanding by just simply
answering a question that you've always wanted to know
or by revealing a future event that would encourage you.
Some people (most people) need to have the Holy Spirit in
their life more to a point of overflowing. He is pouring out
into your life in a new and stronger way right now. In fact, I
am going to tell you a story that happened to me in college
that will undeniably do all the above for you right now. What
happened to the precious individual is beyond comprehension on how much God loves people and wants them to have
His Holy Spirit in an overwhelming, overflowing way!

I remember that this event happened in my second
year of college. During the summers I attended classes and
worked full-time as a security guard at night. There were
times when I would have a couple of weeks off and would
spend that time locked in my room fasting and praying in
the Spirit (tongues). I desired to close out the world and
focus on God. I read out loud whole books of the Bible over
and over again as part of my meditation time. During one
of these sessions, which lasted almost a week, I read the

book of Isaiah for eight hours a day out loud continually (Don't ask me why I just felt that I should do it). One night suddenly I had a strong knowing that I was supposed to stop what I was doing and pick up another book that was written by a spiritual father of mine discussing his supernatural ministry. I opened the book and read aloud again (as I was instructed.) The words in the book disappeared as I read; I could still hear myself reading, but I could no longer see the book. I was taken away in the Spirit to the adjacent property, which was the fairgrounds for that particular city. I could still hear myself reading without missing a word off the pages as I was a half a mile away, standing at the outskirts of the fairgrounds on the sidewalk near a fence. As I stood there facing north, I wondered what the Lord was about to show me because I could not move. It was evening and so I was concerned because it was a bad part of town. All of a sudden I saw a man coming toward me which was uncommon because everyone knows that it's a bad part of town and no one would be walking alone at this time. He was walking rather quickly. A street light revealed he wore a flannel shirt and jeans. As he approached, the Lord caught me away and brought back into my dorm room. I continued reading the book out loud as though I had never left. Interestingly, I returned reading the book in another language. I continued to read in a language unfamiliar to me. The words flowed naturally and fluently; this language out of my own lips but I did not know what I was saying even though I knew it was exactly the same words from the pages, just in another language. It's startled me so I stopped. How could I switch to another language without knowing the language so easily? When I was in the Spirit I flowed in the supernatural language that was not my own, it was as the Spirit gave me utterance: And they were all filled with the Holy Spirit and began to speak with other tongues, as the Spirit gave them utterance (Acts 2:4 emphasis added).

My mind did not understand any of this but the Lord instructed, "Go and witness to this person about My Spirit." I arose from the floor and peered out my window. No one was there, just darkness. So I went to the balcony (I was on the third floor) and looked for a while. No one—of course, it wasn't a safe part of town. I could see a considerable distance. No one was along the fence line of the fairgrounds as far as I could see. The Lord said to me again, "Go and witness to this person about My Spirit and do it now!" So I got myself together and I went down the fire escape (down three floors) and out to the road and walked to the fairgrounds. When I got to the place where I had stood a moment ago, supernaturally, I stopped and said, "See, Lord, there's no one here." He had me look again. There was the man exactly as I had seen him moments before in my room with no way to see out and yet I saw. He wore the same flannel shirt and jeans, and walked swiftly along the fence. I waited until the same scenario that I had seen in the vision happened. I just played it out as though I were an actor. He was about to pass, I quickly walked to intercept him. He became very nervous (as I would have been, having similar feelings about being out in that area). I said, "Hello," to him. He did not stop so I just walked with him. I said, "Well, the Lord has sent me to tell you that there is something to the Holy Spirit and speaking in other languages that are not your own. It is part of the Holy Spirit's process of working in and through you."

I shared with him about the Holy Spirit and he stopped. He asked, "Are you an angel sent to me from the Lord?" I said, "No, I am not angel." He said, "There's no way you can know this but I have been asking the Lord this very question about the Holy Spirit. I have been praying that the Lord would reveal to me if there is an additional experience with the Holy Spirit that I have not encountered yet. My neighbor has been telling me that there is but I was not brought up with those beliefs. You know, about 'speaking in tongues.'"

We continued to walk and I explained the Scriptures to him about the Holy Spirit and the infilling of the Spirit of God, the move of God, prophecy and praying in tongues. He asked me to come to his room at the hotel he was staying. He was a businessman, and was there for a couple days at a convention. He wanted to give me his address so that I could send him material to study and read. I got his address and told him that I would mail him the book I had in my room. We prayed together and I left him there in the hotel room and walked back to dorm room amazed at how God could get to someone when they were asking for help. I found the book and since it was nearing the weekend I decided to mail it the next week on Monday. I continue to seek the Lord in prayer and the next day did the same thing that evening in a similar situation as the previous night. The Lord clearly visited me and told me to take the book that I was going to mail and put it in my pocket and walk miles to the high school and stand in the parking lot.

Once again it was very dark and no one does this in this part of town. But because I was still living off what God had done the previous tonight, I obeyed and walked the distance to high school at night and stood in the parking lot. As I stood in the parking lot for several minutes, a car approached and stopped in front of me. The man from the previous night yelled out at me, "Now I know you're an angel. There is no way you could know that I was still in town. My flight was canceled this morning and had to stay another night and so I was out driving and praying about what you had spoken to me and I was excited to get that book in the mail next week."

I reached in my back pocket and pulled out the book and handed it to him and I said, "Here, the Lord wanted you to have this tonight." At that point he was overwhelmed and asked, "How could you know that I was going be here? You are an angel so what is your real name? You're not human." I said, "The Lord just told me to take your book and come here and stand and wait and so I did. I did not know I was going to see you." So the gentleman took me back to the college campus and said, "Goodbye." I never saw him again, but he was able to encounter *Days of Heaven on Earth* and for that I'm very thankful.

ANGEL VISITATION

Angels are also included in the visitation phase. The angels come and stand beside people and energize (minister to) them! They can cause people to move in the things of God! Manifest miracles, signs and wonders! They minister and provide for the saints. Angels are being sent right now from Heaven, in this phase, because the saints are crying out for visitation.

Angels are part of the Government of God. "Visitation" includes angel encounters. Angels are very bright, fast, and effective in carrying out God's intentions for individuals, groups, and nations. Many angels influence the bringing to pass of God's will. Angels also visit us to protect us. Many can testify of times when angels were involved in protection and supernatural intervention. Angels are secret agents who watch over you as you make the Most High your dwelling place. They will be assigned special missions on your behalf. Here is what the Psalmist says about protection concerning angels:

When we live our lives within the shadow of the God Most High, our secret Hiding Place, we will always be shielded from harm! How then could evil prevail against us, or disease infect us? God sends angels with special orders to protect you wherever you go, defending you from all harm. If you walk into a trap, they'll be there for you and keep you from stumbling! You'll even walk unharmed among the fiercest powers of darkness, trampling every one of them beneath your feet! For here is what the Lord has spoken to me, "Because you have delighted in Me as My great lover, I will greatly protect you. I will set you in a high place, safe and secure before My face. I will answer your cry for help every time you pray, and you will find and feel My presence even in your time of

pressure and trouble. I will be your glorious
Hero and give you a feast! You will be satisfied
with a full life and with all that I do for you.
For you will enjoy the fullness of My salvation"
(Psalm 91:9-16 TPT, emphasis added)!

The Spirit of God has His way and He gets us to a place
where we're consecrated because of revelation, then there
is a process of stronger visitation; more influential and
taking you to the end result, which is habitation. That's the
next phase and that's essentially what's happening to all
of us now.

STEPPING IT UP

When God visits, He starts to step it up. He starts to show
more, but then He requires more.

When He visits, He shows you more. Sometimes it's more
than you think you can handle because it gains access to a
place in your heart that pulls on you. So, you crave Him. You
crave the things of God and you start to assess your life and
your condition and you think, "I want to sell everything and
buy the property where the treasure is; I want to buy the
pearl of great price." Visitation does that.

Thou hast granted me life and favour, and thy visitation hath preserved my spirit (Job 10:12 KJV).

See, revelation is like a first step; it frames your house. Then, God starts to visit you and He starts to reveal parts of Himself – that's what happened with Moses. Moses didn't know God when he was in Egypt. He knew he was from the people of God in a nation that didn't know their God. Moses came to a place where God revealed Himself and His plan of exodus. Moses essentially asked God, "Well, Who do I say sent me? If you're going to tell me to go do this, Who do I say sent me? You know, they've got a million gods. I grew up with this Pharaoh; I've got to know what I'm doing here. They're going to kill me."

God answers Moses, "This is My name: **I Am**." "Ehyeh," is what they pronounced in a covenant. The book of Hebrews reveals that God didn't have anybody to whom He could swear who was greater than He, so He swore by Himself. Well, the whole thing is, "Ehyeh Asher Ehyeh," which is "**I Am that I Am**".

When it comes to our language, words and their meaning can lose their impact from what the truth really is. Everything that God is comes from a realm that has no distance or time. To fully embody the meaning of Who God is with words from a temporal

*realm is difficult. Squeezing an infinite God, an
infinite Kingdom and its infinite attributes into finite
words does not provide a full understanding to us.*

Essentially, before Adam or this universe existed, God was. This truth is conceptually not interpretable.

Whoever God is as a person cannot be put into this language fully. It never will be. The only thing that He could do was squeeze the Word of God into a human body and call His name Emmanuel- Jesus. He revealed as much as He could about Himself to us in 33 years. Through Apostle Paul's teachings and ministry, God gave more revelation of what Jesus did for us. This is how we find out about all of the good things that we have "in Christ".

When Moses went to Pharaoh – think about this – he didn't know God except by the burning bush. He was considered an Israelite, one of the Jewish people. But do you understand they weren't practicing Judaism – there was no temple, there was no tabernacle? Consider the Jewish desert account. God delivered Israel from Egypt. He desired to fellowship with His people. When you read the account you see He wanted them all to come up to the mountain. The Israelites did not want to go. They said to Moses, "You just go up. Whatever He says, we will do. Just go up and find out, and then come back down."

GOD WANTS FELLOWSHIP

I think God was hurt. He said, "Okay, nobody comes near the mountain or they die, including the animals." Am I right? He was hurt. He knew that what He did merited His people's fellowship and intimate worship. Only Moses and Joshua went. Joshua, after they built the tent of meeting, remained and lingered in His presence there constantly (His hunger for God qualified him to be Moses' replacement when Moses died). The Bible teaches that Moses had visitations where he spent weeks at a time on the mountain.

Visitation requires change. Gifts necessitate recip-rocation, which expresses gratitude. He is revealing Himself to you and wants to spend more time with you. Your face is changing with each visitation.

After His lengthy visitations on the mountain, Moses' face starts to change. His face starts to revert back to the original image of Adam, the way Adam looked, the perfect man, when he was face to face with Father God. Moses encountered God's tangible presence. God's presence transformed Moses' face, affecting his features unbeknownst to Moses. When he descended, people feared him because his face glowed. The Bible notes that beams were coming out of his eyes and face. The Israelites demanded he veil his face, hide God's glory.

God called the Israelites stiff-necked because of their resistance to His presence and instruction. He began to resist them in return. God had said, "I'm not going with you. I cannot be with them; I will wipe them out if I am among them." At one point, Moses pled with God, "Listen, You need to cool it. You can't wipe these people out. If you're not going to go with us..." Read it in Chapters 31 through 35 of Exodus. God stopped calling Israel His people and called them Moses' people, "I'm going to send an angel that's going to go before you and he's going to drive out all the inhabitants of the land and he is going to lead your people." At one point, He refers to Israel as, "the people that you lead out." However, He still visited Moses.

Visitations usually include increased angelic activity. When God sent His angel to lead Moses and the Israelites, He cautioned, "Don't grieve him because he won't tolerate your unbelief either, your sin." So, angels don't tolerate our unbelief or purposeful rebellion. Our obedience to God either unleashes or fetters angelic activity in our lives and on our behalf.

I'm telling you all this to try to show you that humanity is in the same spot. We are getting to the place where God is visiting us, but He requires us to change and yield so we increase our influence and effectiveness. If you doubt what I suggest, look at what the writer of Hebrews writes, "Listen, and don't be like they were in the desert where they fell. Don't be like them. Enter in by yielding to Him."

Hebrews reflects the Exodus in some facets. The writer implores us, "Don't through unbelief, be like the children of Israel who fell in the desert after God had done all of that for them." I mean, he's talking to believers, but he's using the example of Israel's stiff-neckedness.

When God changes you, the change translates into your relationships. Some folk simply will not be comfortable. Just as the Israelites asked Moses to veil his face, you will experience people resisting God's glory in you. Some people resist because they don't want to change, some resist simply because of doubt. I know of people that are encountering visitations of Jesus that didn't even believe in Him until He appeared to them (which is what happened to Paul on the road to Damascus).

MEETING WITH GOD

God had Moses build a tent of meeting where people could enter in the presence of the Lord. There is no indication anybody went there except for Joshua and Moses. Scripture records that Moses and Joshua would get up and go, but Israel would come to the doors of their tents and stand there and watch him enter, and wait for him to finish. Then, they wanted Moses to veil God's glory.

Visitation is available to everyone. Some people are just looking at it from outside, and some people want to participate in it. *No one should just tolerate it.*

During the transition from revelation to visitation, people may resist or run from God's revealed Glory, and the demand it places on them. In churches there are Children of God desiring and crying out for the supernatural and visitation; and then there are people who simply resist God, the reasons are many.

Jesus is supernatural and the Holy Spirit is supernatural. There's nothing about God that is normal as far as human beings are concerned on the level that we live, because we're in a fallen world. If your business is normal, then there's something wrong. I don't mean that in a bad way. When God is allowed entrance into the various facets of life and heart chambers, His supernatural supersedes the natural in those areas where He has been permitted to reign. Supernatural things happen in your business. You have supernatural things happen in everything that you do because you've invited Him in and He's

visiting you. When He visits you, there is a change.
Even your face shows it.

Soon God's glory permeates your sphere of influence: the workplace, home place, marketplace, etc. Corporately, His glory transcends from the prayer room to the congregation. The congregation may not realize the labor in the prayer room. The homework is done; it was done by 15 people that most people don't even know exist or don't realize were just in that room or maybe just stayed up all night at their house because they couldn't stop praying. For those who are a part of prayer, when you see the glory manifest in church, you apprehend, "Oh, that's what was going on in prayer." People start catching on fire, without knowing who lit the match. They just know it's been a good service, that it wasn't normal.

When God shows up, it's not normal. However, there is accountability when you receive from God. In Moses' tent of meeting, the people didn't take advantage of God's presence. Yet, the people that did were changed. We must choose to avail ourselves to His presence. There is a deeper manifestation of God available to us. Moses said, "Show me Your Glory." Wait a minute. He said, "Glory," not "presence"? God had just said, "My presence will go with you," but God didn't use the word that Moses sought. Moses placed a demand on

God, "No, I want to see Your Glory." I always had wondered about that.

I found that glory is a part of God that He veils. It's a part of God that He chose not to reveal until He gave His Son, Who is the exact image of the Father. But when the Glory is manifested on God or Jesus, something happens to His face that I encountered where I was not allowed to look. You can have God's presence and everything is fine. And you can have God's Glory as long as it doesn't start to come out of His face. Because when it comes to the face, there is something so beyond my ability to describe to you that is revealed that you cannot live to tell about it. I know that's hard for a lot of people to accept. But I have experienced being with Jesus but not being able to look at His face (of Jesus) when the Glory manifested. When the glory of God began to beam through His face, man was not permitted to see the face of God in that state and live. I encountered the fear of the Lord because I realized that He was so much more than I could take. I'm just telling you, because this happened to me, I am convinced that there's parts of God that we will not see; we can't handle it. But we can still experience being in His presence during it.

I saw myself in my glorified state, on the other side
of the veil, and I could hardly look at myself. The

perfection that was on me was to the point where I could hardly stand it. And that's just me. I've seen angel faces that I could hardly stand, they were so beautiful. I've seen Jesus's face to where I didn't want to look away. There have been times when what was on Him was so holy and so sacred and so separate, that He was beyond what I could handle.

CHAPTER 7

Phase Three: Habitation

 ❧

J esus shared with me the 3rd and final phase of *"Days of Heaven on Earth"* is *"Habitation."* There is a place where the Spirit of the Lord can take you to where your whole spiritual house has been framed by revelation from God, and then it has been ornamented with visitation and now you are being occupied with habitation. And it's permanent. We see there is a part of God, His face, where Moses was not permitted to see when His Glory was in full manifestation. What Moses did see was enough. The Glory of God was different from the presence. Habitation, when God dwells with you, is beyond the acquaintance (or visitation) stage. We will never know the end of Him. Habitation has to do with having so much in common in your heart with Him that you don't get in the way.

A FACIAL: OF THE GOD KIND

Habitation is a place where He has won you over and your face is glowing and it doesn't bother you. You don't even know it, but it's affecting other people and some may be feeling a bit uncomfortable with the place you have gone in Him. Jesus has taken you to a place where you have so much in common with Him. You have become like Him and you don't even know that you are not really normal any more to some people. Your face is glowing and people can't look at you.

Whenever Moses went out to the Tent of Meeting, all the people would get up and stand in their tent entrances. They would all watch Moses until he *disappeared* inside. As he went into the tent, the pillar of cloud would come down and hover at the entrance while the LORD spoke with Moses. Then all the people would stand and bow low at their tent entrances. Inside the Tent of Meeting, the LORD would speak to *Moses face to face*, as a man speaks to his friend. Afterward Moses would return to the camp, but the young man who assisted him, Joshua son of Nun, stayed behind in the Tent of Meeting (Exodus 33:8-11 NLT, emphasis added).

When Moses came down the mountain carrying the stone tablets inscribed with the terms of the covenant, he wasn't aware that his face glowed because he had spoken to the LORD face to face. And when Aaron and the people of Israel saw the *radiance of Moses' face, they were afraid to come near him* (Exodus 34:29-30 NLT, emphasis added).

That old system of law etched in stone led to death, yet it began with such *glory* that the people of Israel could not bear to look at Moses' *face*. For his face shone with the glory of God, even though the *brightness* was already fading away. Shouldn't we expect far *greater glory* when the Holy Spirit is giving life? If the old covenant, which brings condemnation, was glorious, how much more glorious is the new covenant, which makes us right with God! In fact, that first glory was not glorious at all compared with the *overwhelming glory* of the new covenant. So if the old covenant, which has been set aside, was full of glory, then the new covenant, which remains forever, has far *greater glory* (2 Corinthians 3:7-11 NLT, emphasis added).

Once, someone mistreated me continually. I finally asked, "What is your problem?" He replied, "Every time I get around you, I just feel like I need to get on my knees and confess all my sins to you." Surprised, I questioned, "What?" He clarified, "I don't know. There's something around you, I feel so convicted that I feel like I should confess my sins to you." I explained, "Well, that's not me." He had felt *Who* was with me, not me personally.

You see, whom *you bring with you affects your environment. When Jesus Lives with you and in you, then your environment is impacted and transformed for the Kingdom of Heaven.*

People can be impacted by *His Presence* in your presence. I realized that it was the fact that I was in the *Habitation phase,* dwelling and yielding to *His Presence. You* can see His influence on others during this phase. My heart has been captured by Him. He had expanded His domain over and through me. He is not a respecter of persons. He longs to do this for everyone.

When you spend time with Jesus, He gently teaches you, until you are transformed and habitable. Your habitation has become clean and well ornamented, no longer

contaminated by unholy activities and thoughts. He is
better than any earthly housekeeper.

Paul writes in I Corinthians 10:23, " All things are legitimate [permissible—and we are free to do anything we
please], but not all things are helpful (expedient, profitable,
and wholesome). All things are legitimate, but not all things
are constructive [to character] and edifying [to spiritual life]
(AMP)." As you grow in Him, the Holy Spirit will fine tune
you. He will begin to purge you of the practices that do not
benefit or edify your growth. Your relationship with Him will
increase your influence in the Kingdom. God desires that not
one soul would perish. He desires that we reconcile those
precious people to Him within our realm of influence. When
an activity or thought pattern doesn't strengthen or benefit
our realm of influence or redirect others to Kingdom Life as
well, then it has to go.

It's time to fall in love. When you grow intimate with
Him, your desires become His desires. If you do not
desire the things He wants, it's time for a healthy
dose of "Heavenly Reality" from the Spirit of Truth.

I HAVE A YOKE FOR YOU

You get to the place where the Lord says, "Take My yoke upon you." You don't even hesitate because Jesus has won your heart. He has pursued and over-taken because you yielded. You are overwhelmed in Habitation.

Jesus offers to all who are willing:

Come to Me, all you who labor and are heavy laden, and I will give you rest. Take My yoke upon you and learn from Me, for I am gentle and lowly in heart, and you will find rest for your souls. For My yoke is easy and My burden is light" (Matthew 11:28-30).

Jesus taught me that the reason why God the Father was telling the Israelites all the time, in the desert, they were stiff-necked was because they weren't yielding. *They weren't yielding to the yoke.* The term stiff-necked came up a lot and it had to do with the fact that it means unyielding, stubborn. I realized that if I want habitation then I am going to have to yield to a place where I have the same heart as God.

In addition to sharing my heart with God, I must recognize and yield to Who He is and who I am not. Jesus was promoted as King over the entire universe; we are seated with Him in Heavenly places. But without Him; forget it, we are not even mentionable, we are "but dust" (please see Ephesians 2:6 and Psalm 103:14).

When I met Jesus, I realized that because of His personality, He had made a way for me to have this supernatural transition; He had made a way for *everyone* to come up to the mountain and not only visit with God, but live with Him; God dwells among men and He has a Kingdom. I realized that He has given me the Kingdom. He has entrusted the *Body* of believers, which includes you and me, with everything related to the Kingdom realm and its advance.

> *If you want to do something that's not part of what*
> *His goal or purpose is, then there's going to be dis-*
> *crepancies. There's not going to be the unity because*
> *there are different levels of relationship and commit-*
> *ment. Habitation is one of those levels where you just*
> *have to be on the same page.*

When you are on the same page with Him in the *Habitation phase*, the relationship dynamics with God elevate beyond what you have ever encountered. In my personal walk, He has said, "You know what? I'm going to go out and minister to people. Can I have your body? I'm going to go out and feed the poor. Do you have any food that I can take to give out?" He starts asking, "Can I borrow your car? Can I borrow your bank card? Can I borrow your business? Can I borrow your friends?" I realized I'm getting it.

I started to realize that habitation was God building a place to dwell, and that place was me. He was working to gain access.

We are all called to the ministry of reconciliation in 2 Corinthians 5. We're called to compel people to come in and be reconciled to God. He wants to create a dwelling place among His people. For the most part, people are stiff-necked and in unbelief; how greatly they need to be reconciled to our Father! We have to go out and *win people's hearts.* We can accomplish this call when we allow Him to govern our lives, our bodies, our lips, and our ears. Through our yielding, the Holy Spirit will operate in words of knowledge, wisdom and prophecy, as well as in discerning of spirits so that when we go out, the Holy Spirit equips us to reach each person in our destined paths with *exactly their hearts' cries.* We're at work with Him everywhere, not just in church. When we are fully yielded to God flowing through us, all of our provisions will be there. Amazing, supernatural things will start happening.

He starts to have influence over you as you come to terms with Him. He wants you to see things from where He stands and from His perspective, which is higher than ours (see Isaiah 55:9).

I NEED TO BORROW YOU

I would like to share with you a very amazing experience that I had. In the summer of 1986, I had already graduated in the spring with my bachelor's degree; I had been fasting on and off and praying continually for approximately three years beginning in the second year of college and ending shortly after this experience. For that last year I had been led to skip my dinner every day. There were times when I would pray in the Spirit (tongues) so long and deeply that I could not transition back to English. I yielded to the Spirit in times of prayer for days at a time without eating a single meal during the summer months. I always missed dinner during the school year. After graduation, I took summer classes in the morning and spent the remaining time praying, several hours a day on average. Most of this was done in the Spirit—praying in a heavenly language which was not my own known language. I prayed out loud for hours without stopping.

1 Corinthians 14:14-16 explains:

> For if I pray in a tongue, my spirit prays, but my understanding is unfruitful. What is the conclusion then? I will pray with the spirit, and I will also pray with the understanding. I will sing with the spirit, and I will also sing with the understanding.

One morning, I was finishing a session of prayer, I felt the Lord prompt me to sing to Him, *Amazing Grace,* which I knew very well. But it wasn't that easy. He asked me to sing it to Him in the Spirit; to sing in languages unknown to me, being led and inspired by the Spirit. My thinly walled dorm housed many students and I knew that people would hear me. I didn't feel quite comfortable with that, but I felt the Lord compelling me, so I did. I sang *Amazing Grace* in tongues. Even though it was in a language that I did not know, its sound was beautiful and familiar. The anointing hit me so strong that I forgot about people hearing me. I sang, exerting my voice loudly as though in a concert hall. I am compelled to believe the Spirit sent my song forth like a prophecy.

Resolved that I had fulfilled the Lord's request, I relaxed into my next project. Almost immediately, a knock sounded at my door, concerning me because I was really loud and I knew that I probably disturbed someone. I opened my door slightly. A young man introduced himself to me. Through the cracked door, the young man explained that he was a missionary's son from the Yucatán peninsula sent to go to college in town. He wanted to meet me because I was singing *Amazing Grace* in his dialect from the Yucatán peninsula. He wanted to know what town I had grown up in because I had the same dialect as he did, which was rare. I looked at him shocked and I wondered if he was joking. He was very serious and was crying. I knew he wasn't kidding. I told him that I know no other language except English and that I had never been to the Yucatán peninsula. He said, 'That's impossible because you just sang *Amazing Grace* in my dialect perfectly." He further explained that some of the words, which were more difficult, were pronounced very well.

At this point I asked him to come in because he was really crying and I thought that I needed to hear his whole story. He told me that he had grown-up down in Central America and that his parents had felt he should go to Bible school for training. He was sent to a school in town which was about

20 minutes away from my college. He told me that while he was at this college, the Spirit of the Lord came upon him and he spoke in tongues (other languages) as known in the Bible. The bottom line was that the college of that particular movement or denomination does not agree with the Holy Spirit operating that way today. I guess he got reported and they dismissed him from the college for doctrine conflicts. He was heartbroken because he felt that he let his parents down. Rather than go back to the Yucatán, he had discovered my college believed the Holy Spirit operated this way today. He applied and got into the college and had just moved in across the hallway from me. He was praying and felt damaged by all that happened. He had just sat down when all of a sudden he heard *Amazing Grace* being sung in his native language. So when he came over to talk to me he was excited because he felt God had given him a friend (me) that was from the same exact region that he was from. But it was a far greater act of love than that from the Lord. Through this experience, God confirmed to him the authenticity of his walk with God and the present day ministry of the Holy Spirit.

Ending the account here would be enough to encourage anyone. But it was only the beginning. For the next week, I would see him every day and I would sense the Holy Spirit wanting to speak out loud through me. So I began to yield to what God was doing. I spoke in the most fluent Spanish for days and he interpreted. I was amazed at how the Holy Spirit was covering specific events in the future, even names and places, and events that had to take place but would not happen unless I prayed them out and gained a certain degree of understanding from my spirit (inner man) to my soul (mind will, and emotions). In some cases, the Holy Spirit was saying (in fluent Spanish) that I was behind schedule on some events, and that there were specific people waiting for me to arrive at their location. I was holding up progress and it affected other people! Through this process of this supernatural experience, we found the Holy Spirit telling me that I was to be in Tulsa yesterday! So we called the bus station and got a ticket for me to go to Tulsa, OK. That morning at about three, the Spirit was also saying, in perfect Spanish, that I already had a job, car, place to stay, and would be attending a 2yr training program at a local college for ministry preparation; giving the name of the college and its location. I knew this college and wanted to attend it. The supernatural thing about it was that this guy did not know any of this. He was just translating what I was saying in my prayer language and telling me.

I was taken by this missionary's son to the bus station that next morning. We said our goodbyes and I took one of the last seats next to a young lady. The lady was attending her second year at the same college that the Spirit of God told me I was going to attend in the fall. She reassured me and offered to help in any way possible. When we got to Tulsa she gave me a ride to Oral Roberts University where I felt I should go next. From there I was taken by a man I met who was a security guard for the campus. He happened to know where a friend of mine lived that was my Hall counselor at the college I had just graduated. He had already graduated a year ago. The Lord was leading me every step of the way and when I arrived at his residence, His leading was obvious. It was as though God had sent him and his wife ahead to Tulsa just for me. I knocked on the door with my luggage and they answered. They were so helpful and asked if I needed a place to live because they had a big house. I said, "Yes!" He then said that he had a position open at his company and offered me a job. I was working at my new job by five pm that day. I was able to ride with him every day to work. I eventually got a car supernaturally that was paid in full. I attended the college for two years and graduated in 1987, just as the Spirit had spoken. It was a heavenly encounter that involved a foreign language that I was able to speak supernaturally.

I was deeply touched by the way the Lord reached out to this individual. God's ultimate goal in habitation is to include you in on what He is doing on the earth in the lives of others. I was able to see this in action and still see it happen today.

WHEN TRINITY PURSUES YOU

When you make the decision to love God with all your heart and obey all that He commands, He is able to move in with you. Obviously the criterion has been met through the precious Blood of Jesus that was shed. It's just a matter of time now, so you might as well give up on resisting any longer. The Lord is much too strong for you and you know you want to be caught by Him. Up until this point, you have been pursuing God by asking Him for *Revelation*. He accommodates you through the Holy Spirit and answers your prayers based on the Apostle Paul's prayers in the letters to the Ephesians, and Colossians (see Ephesians 1:17–23; Colossians 1:9-23). He begins to frame you as a house would be framed using these beautiful beams of *Revelation*, revealing Himself through His Word to you.

Next, He begins to come to you through *Visitation*. As you enter this phase, you desire to know Him even more. The more He visits the more you desire Him to visit. It gets to where you want Him to stay! You pursue Him until *Habitation* comes.

At this point, He turns around in the middle of you pursuing Him and He lets you catch Him. Then, He begins to pursue you and you can't escape Him. You see, Jesus is irresistible to you, but what you did not know was that you became irresistible to Him and now He pursues you! Welcome to Habitation!

Paul describes this journey well when he says:

> And you, who once were alienated and enemies in your mind by wicked works, yet now He has reconciled in the body of His flesh through death, *to present you holy, and blameless, and above reproach in His sight*—if indeed you continue in the faith, grounded and steadfast, and are not moved away from the hope of the gospel which you heard, which was preached to every creature under heaven, of which I, Paul, became a minister (Colossians 1:19-23, emphasis added);

Also in Ephesians 2:19-22:

> Now therefore ye are no more strangers and foreigners, but fellow citizens with the saints, and

of the household of God; And are built upon the foundation of the apostles and prophets, Jesus Christ himself being the chief corner stone; In whom all *the building fitly framed together growth unto an holy temple in the Lord: In whom ye also are builded together for an habitation of God through the Spirit (KJV emphasis added).*

WORDS ARE WHO YOU ARE

The Spirit is where there's freedom, but the Spirit has lines. The Spirit has rules of engagement. He doesn't go beyond what's been spoken, because the Spirit and the Word are congruent, and essentially the same to God. The reason I want to show you this is because in our culture, there often is discrepancy between a person's word and who they are as a person. With God, there is no difference between what He says and Who He is. What He says is the same as Who He is; when He says something, He's good for it. It's Who He is as a person, and He would never separate Himself from what He says. We don't know that down here. We don't know people by their word. We think, "Well, that's what they say," realizing that often what is said doesn't happen. This ought not to be. A person is not supposed to be any different from their word. Who they are as a person is what they say. There's no discrepancy in Heaven. We must learn to align our words with the Word.

We don't know God correctly because we don't understand Him – like your name; what your name means is who you are. God isn't just faithful. Revelation prophesies "a white horse, whose rider (Jesus) is called Faithful and True" (Revelation 19:11). "Faithful and True" comprise not only His name, but Who He is as a person. You can't separate the fact that He's faithful from His actual name. Who God is as a person is what He says and what He does, and there's no difference. We don't experience that concept down here. We say we know God by His Word, but His Word and He are the same. There's no difference. What He says is no different than who He is. If He told you something, you might as well just go to the bank with what He said, because there's no difference between Who He is as a person and what He's told you. He's good for it. I realize I am being repetitive, but this truth is *vital* for your growth with God.

Remember when I said that when you give up everything for God, you gain everything for God? When you reach the place of Habitation, you will experience God prospering you in every facet of life that you yield to Him.

Prosperity is something that God does for us, because we have been displaced by Him. Since He is

131

prosperous, since He is healthy, He is perfect. When He shows up, it pushes out infirmity, it pushes out poverty, it pushes out all these things; they're displaced. It's not something that I do but how much I yield to Him. I don't have to convince God of something that He already is:

I AM

CHAPTER 8

Enoch, the Bride, and the Church Age

◈

THE POWERS OF THE COMING AGE

The powers of the coming age are mentioned in Hebrews:

> For it is impossible for those who were once enlightened, and have tasted the Heavenly gift, and have become partakers of the Holy Spirit, and have tasted the good Word of God and *the powers of the age to come*, if they fall away, to renew them again to repentance, since they crucify again for themselves the Son of God, and put Him to an open shame (Heb. 6:4-6 NKJV, emphasis added).

AN ANGEL ESCORT

I always wondered about what was being said here. I asked the Lord, "What are the powers of the coming age?" The Word says that we've experienced the powers of coming age. I sought the Lord for understanding of that passage of scripture. The Lord answered me with an amazing encounter.

On October 16th, a couple of years ago on my wife Kathi's birthday, we were on an airplane traveling to Seattle. I had on my headsets. I was on the aisle seat in the airplane, and someone came and stood beside me in the aisle. I opened my eyes and the power of God hit me. Initially, I did not see anybody; suddenly, I saw an angel standing in the aisle beside me. He grabbed me and took me, and we left the airplane. We traveled fast. He had me by the arm and away we went. We landed where a forest opened to a field. I did not know where we were. I saw a man who was pretty short walking on the path in front of us. He wore a garment which reminded me of an animal skin.

The angel spoke, "I've been given permission to show you the powers of the coming age." He said, "Watch!" He pointed to the man as he took one more step. The resurrection power just burst around him as he stepped from the earthly realm into the Heavenly realm. His name was Enoch. The power that came out from him as he stepped into the Heavenly realm was so strong, that it hit both me and the angel; bursting right through us. The burst was bright and powerful. Then the angel said, "Come." He took me and we went to another place very fast. I saw another man standing (Elijah), and a chariot came and he got in it. The same thing happened - there was a burst of resurrection power. The same power that raised Jesus from the dead, burst around him and he disappeared. The blast came back and hit us once again. It was so strong! Then the angel turned to me and handed me a scroll which I do not have because it is in the Bible. He said, "You need to read II Corinthians, chapter 5, especially verse 17. You have been called to a ministry of reconciliation. You've been shown the powers of the coming age so that you can participate in it right now." He said, "People just need to be told that they have been bought, that all of humanity has been bought and purchased. They just need to be told that it's already been paid for. You tell them that God has pur-chased them through Jesus Christ, and this is the powers of the coming age." He then took me back to 40,000 feet, put me in my seat on the right airplane and left.

MINISTRY OF RECONCILIATION

It's the ministry of reconciliation! The resurrection is so strong that when you testify, it raises people from the dead and they come back to life right before your eyes as you announce this good news to them. It was explained to me why the testimony of Jesus is the Spirit of Prophecy:

> And I fell at his feet to worship him. But he said to me, "See that you do not do that! I am your fellow servant, and of your brethren who have the testimony of Jesus. Worship God for the testimony of Jesus is the Spirit of Prophecy" (Revelation 19:10 NKJV)!

> *When you start to talk about Jesus, it gets into prophecy because the Spirit wants to testify and take over. When you start talking about Jesus, the Holy Spirit automatically manifests every time.*

I realized that the resurrection power that is dwelling in me wants to raise people from the dead. I can spiritually raise people from the dead just by testifying of Jesus; it initiates that resurrection power. It's a function of the ministry of reconciliation. The angel had given me a scroll but I did not have it when I returned. The scroll contained the entire fifth chapter of II Corinthians, which the angel said I needed to learn. He said, "You need to learn the whole chapter, especially in the area of verses 15 and 17."

For the love of Christ compels us, because we judge thus: that if One died for all, then all died; and He died for all, that those who live should live no longer for themselves, but for Him who died for them and rose again. Therefore, from now on, we regard no one according to the flesh. Even though we have known Christ according to the flesh, yet now we know Him thus no longer. Therefore, if anyone is in Christ, he is a new creation; old things have passed away; behold, all things have become new. Now all things are of God, who has reconciled us to Himself through Jesus Christ, and has given us the *ministry of reconciliation*, that is, that God was in Christ reconciling the world to Himself, not imputing their trespasses to them, and has committed to us the word of reconciliation. Now then, we are ambassadors for Christ, as though God were pleading through us: we implore you on Christ's behalf, be reconciled to God. For He made Him who knew no sin to be sin for us, that we might become the righteousness of God in Him (2 Corinthians 5:14-21 emphasis added).

THE LIFE AND MINISTRY OF ENOCH

We have discussed revelation, visitation, and habitation. Now we are examining Enoch.

Here are some facts about him. Enoch:

1. lived 365 years;
2. started walking with God at age 65;
3. walked with God 300 years;
4. was a prophet who prophesied (see Jude 14);
5. pleased God and was taken away with Him (see Heb.11:5);
6. was born into the 7th generation from Adam (see Jude 14).

"As were the days of Noah, so will be the coming of the Son of Man" (Matthew 24:37 AMP).

The parallel to this is that Enoch was caught away. He walked with God and he was not. So shall be the Church. The Church is in the Church Age, a dispensation where God focuses on His Body through the Church. We are in the Church Age today. Change is coming where the Church Age dispensation ends. The transition of ages parallels the life and ministry of Enoch.

The Bride is getting ready. Enoch, the Bride, and this
church age each have significance right now. You
see, at any one point during a year, a bride could see
the groom come in the Jewish wedding. They were
betrothed for a year. Anytime during that year, he
could suddenly come for her.

So, parameters of a Jewish groom's arrival for his bride relates with everything which we currently experience. We get to the place where we walk with God and we're not, because we become a Bride that pleases God so much, that God will take us and catch His Bride away. It's not a time to shrink back. It's not a time to fear. It's time to look up. That is where we find ourselves right now, with the expectation for the Spirit and the Bride to beckon in unison, "Come." The Spirit and the Bride will say the same thing. And when the Spirit is able to manifest Himself in the Bride that much to where the Bride says the same thing, Jesus will come back. Quickly! (Revelation 22:17) That is what Jesus told me, "The secret is that the Spirit and the Bride say 'Come.'" That's the desired and required oneness.

Jesus wants to coach us. He says, "You know, I really
want you to ask me for something right now."

He wants us to ask Him. He wants to teach us something that we're not getting. He wants to coach us. That is the kind of person that Jesus is; the person that I met. This is the person who died for me. He is the kind of person that God the Father cannot tell when Jesus is returning because Jesus would tell us. Think about it. Why does Jesus not know when He is coming back? Why is it that only the Father knows? I'm telling you, I've met Him; He would tell us (see Mark 13:32).

I realized that I had not made room for Him. I asked Him to let the Holy Spirit reveal this all to me, I was not asking for that enough through those prayers in Ephesians and Colossians. But also, during the visitations, I wasn't yielding to the truth that He was relaying to me through the visitations, and change is required each time He visits, whether if He comes in a service, during prayer, or in a believer's meeting. The exchange rate must be satisfied – the revelation He dispenses during His visit necessitates transformation in and through us.

He wants us to get to the place where we have habitation, that we have so much in common, that He stays. He decides He is not going to go home, His home is in the Church individually and corporately. Then He says, "I'm going to feed the poor, do you want to come? Can I borrow you? I'm going to visit some people that are in jail or I'm going to go to work with you today because I want to talk to someone. Can I borrow you?"

I realize my focus needed "revelation help" – I was focusing on the Tabernacle of David, Temple of Solomon, the Holy of Holies, the Secret Place, the Cleft of the Rock, and if I could just find that Ark of the Covenant! The whole time, what He wanted was *Days of Heaven on Earth for me* through *habitation.* That is what He bought for us. He wants to live in and through us.

I discovered the three stages: Revelation, Visitation, and Habitation were exactly what He had intended for me and you all along. He wanted a dwelling place and He wants it to be among you and me. God seeks a people that will yield and let Him show His glory through them, manifesting with signs and wonders and everything that is a part of Him as a person. When He is welcome fully in our hearts, *Heaven on Earth* will start happening in our lives. As I tell you this, please know its correction time for me, too. Do you realize that if the supernatural is not happening, it's not God's fault because supernatural is just the way He is as a person? Supernatural is His natural. When He shows up, supernatural things are going to happen.

People ask me, "When did you become like this?" or "Where have you been?" I say, "I have been this way since I was 19, I became this way when I gave my life to Him." They often respond, "You're kidding?" I reply, "I have been this way." That is to say, I am not the way I am simply because the book was released. I have walked a consistent walk from my spiritual birthday. If you're going to pinpoint a place where it happened, it was the day I fully surrendered to Him. Interestingly, God sought me before I was born again. I have had supernatural events occur since I was 10 years old. If you inventory your life, you'll realize that you had supernatural things happening, too. God is not a respecter of persons.

I just wanted to close with this: Angel activity is and will continue to increase so strongly that they are going to actually be better friends than your earthly friends are at times.

Angels will become more help than some of your friends. They are just as real as people, but they're even more real because they are full of truth, and truth is eternal. They're a lot smarter, a lot brighter; they've got it together. They see the face of God and worship Him, then they come down to help you. They can really help transform the atmosphere because they came from the ultimate worship center of the universe!

PENTAGON BRIEFING

How this all started with me was back in December right before the turn of the year here, the end of '14, and the beginning of this year, '15. On December 6, 2014, I was told to go to Washington D.C. I stayed a night in the Doubletree Hotel across from the Pentagon. When I did, I had six angels show up and give me instruction. I thought, "Who is ever going to believe me, that this is actually happening?" I was trying to picture myself telling somebody this. "There's just no way that I'm ever going to convince someone that this happened."

Everything they told me has happened. Everything to the "t" has happened perfectly.

I watched it happen in my church. I watched it happen in my life. I've watched it happen with everything. It was so perfect. But the one thing they told me was, "Kevin, you get it. That is why when we heard you were coming, we couldn't wait to talk to you because you get it and we know that you're going to drop everything that you're doing to participate in this. You're not going to wait for this move of God that it's already here. You're going to start seeing it in your church." This was in December. "You're going to start seeing miracles. You're going to start seeing the manifestation of God. Be obedient."

These angels said, "Listen, we were given these sacred things and sent down here to give these to you. These books are sacred; they're on a bookshelf in Heaven. Your testimony is already written." They showed me how they do it. There's a veil. They just took these beautiful gold ornamented boxes that are gifts from God. They passed them through the veil, instructing, "Take them." I took them into my hand. They said, "These are for you. No one else is to touch them."

Then they said, "Can you just raise your hands and worship God? We just love it when you worship God with no music. You do not even need music or anything; you just lift your hands and you start worshipping God as though you're at the Throne." So, I did. I started worshipping. They all raised their hands and worshipped with me. I pondered, "Is this really happening?" They request, "Can you just worship God like you do? We just love it how you can worship God without having music or anything." I guess it's something special that happens that is released through us as human beings that is different to God than the angels, because the angels worship all the time. Worship is part of what they do. They're always worshipping, they're always joyful, and they're always excited about what God is doing. They're trying to relay their fervor and passion for God and His Kingdom to us down here, but they do not achieve results as quickly with everyone. They are persistent to see it through, they want God's plan fulfilled for each of us. When angels find people that respond and do what's right, they congregate. You can attract their activity. They look for people who desire to participate in what's coming.

Angels are looking for people that will actually just start participating in the move now, before it even goes to full manifestation, people like you and me who will just start to walk in it now. Angels come around you and make it so much easier. They will help you to the point where other people will wonder how you're doing what you're doing, and it will be because God has shown favor on you; all because you have chosen to allow Him to come in. These angels can do so much. They are here to help.

There is much written about us not yet fulfilled, because it's so much more than we've comprehended. That is why Paul wrote to the Corinthians. He said that it hasn't even entered into your mind, that ear has not heard, eye has not seen what God has planned for those who love Him, that you cannot comprehend it:

But, on the contrary, as the Scripture says, What eye has not seen and ear has not heard and has not entered into the heart of man, [all that] God has prepared (made and keeps ready) for those who love Him [who hold Him in affectionate reverence, promptly obeying

Him and gratefully recognizing the bene-
fits He has bestowed] [Isaiah 64:4; 65:17] (1
Corinthians 2:9 AMP).

HEALED BECAUSE YOU ASKED

I found there are things that have happened for me that
would not have automatically occurred – Jesus said, "I just
want you to know that if you had not asked Me for that, it
would not have happened." When I asked Jesus to heal me –
the doctors couldn't help me, but I was healed immediately.
The next morning I awoke and I did not have three ailments
that had plagued me. Do you know what else He said to me?
I was healed of these things and He said, "You're not asking
for enough; you did not ask for enough." I said, "Okay, I want
this, this, and this." And He said, "Okay." Then it started happening. I mean, one of them is impossible and it's happening
right now. You'll see it in a few months. I already saw the
future. I have already been there. He said, "If you hadn't
asked Me for this, it wouldn't have happened. You would
have never known it was available to you." And I'm thinking,
"You just told me I wasn't asking enough. You just coached
me to ask you for this ridiculous request that is impossible."
And it's happening. He reiterated, "The only reason its happening is because you asked Me." And I told Him, "Well, the

only reason I asked You is because You coached me." How wonderfully gracious is He!?

I share all of this because the healings reflect the personality of Jesus. The book focuses on the personality of Jesus. I considered all of the aspects that I could think of that the Spirit was telling me to concentrate on about Jesus. He is a *person* and not a religious figure in a church. I realized He is the type of person with whom *you would want to "hang out"*, but your relationship with Him cannot go any further than your "yielded submission" to Him. He is a very strong personality, an aspect I miss most about the Jesus Whom I met when on the other side of the veil during my *Heavenly Visitation.*

The Jesus Whom I met was thorough and direct, admonishing, "Listen, if you want to wrap this up the right way, if you want to be more than just written down in the Lamb's Book of Life, if *you want to be one of the pillars, to be right in there with Me for eternity*, to keep on going and be shoulder-to-shoulder with Me for eternity, then Love Me by doing My word right now!" That is *strong*!

You'll search for every impossible situation you can
and you put yourself in the middle of it. When it
doesn't look like you're going to make it, you keep
breathing in Heaven. When you can't handle a

person, you continue to pray for them. You continue to do what you feel you can't do because the Lord has secured a spot for you in the new Kingdom that is already progressing right now. You are effective and valuable!

EXTRA OIL

We have to allow ourselves to be placed in the future millennial Kingdom right now. Get the extra oil in your lamps *now*. You see, the extra oil is this: tomorrow when you wake up, you're a thousand years ahead in your supply. I know that sounds crazy, but I'm not just saying it. Oil is what you need to burn and be a light. So get more than enough and burn brightly in and for Him. Oil is being delivered by the Holy Spirit daily to your doorstep from Heaven.

Conclusion

Jesus can take you to a place where you're way beyond your years. You're way beyond what people have planned for you. You're way beyond what you have planned for you. You're way beyond any and all of what can be imagined by the carnal mind. You have the capacity to do the impossible, and the only reason why is because you have allowed Jesus to talk to you and influence you as a person. Let the next step be the one that places you in your Days of Heaven on Earth!

Author's Note

Please look for the companion study guide that will be offered in the near future for personal and group Bible Studies.

CPSIA information can be obtained
at www.ICGtesting.com
Printed in the USA
BVHW04s1401190718
521945BV00034B/686/P

9 781498 448215